COSMIC DIAGRAMS

SPIRALS, FRACTALS, ISLAMIC PATTERNS, LABYRINTHS, MANDALAS

BY MILENA

M PUBLISHING

CONTENTS

SPIRALS 4
FRACTALS 14
LABYRINTHS 30
COSMIC DIAGRAMS 38
ENDNOTES 45
BIBLIOGRAPHY 47

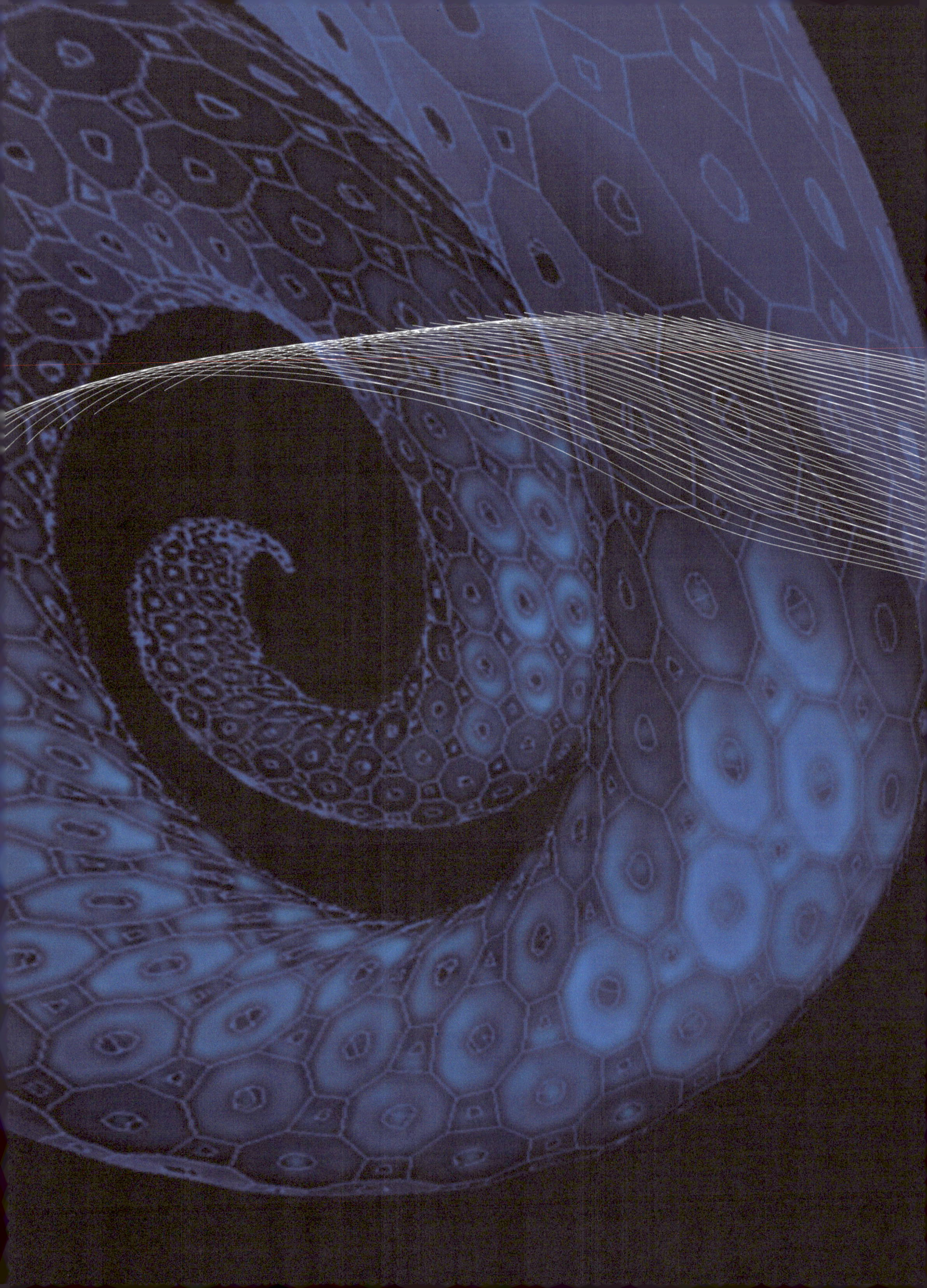

SPIRALS

THE EYE OF THE SPIRAL	5
GOLDEN AND FIBONACCI SPIRALS	7
SPIRALS IN THE PLANT WORLD	8
PHYLLOTAXIS	10
OTHER LIVING SPIRALS	10
BEYOND THE ORGANIC WORLD	11
SYMBOL OF AN INNER GROWTH	12

1.1 – Continuously diminishing golden rectangles converge toward a never-reachable point – the eye of the golden spiral

THE EYE OF THE SPIRAL

The spiral is a line that curves around a fixed point at a continually changing distance. There are numerous ways to make that journey. Figure 1.4 shows three examples of spiral geometry. In the second one, we can notice that the spiral path is being mapped by the addition of ever enlarging segments made up of self-similar triangles. That way, the size of the spiral increases while the shape remains similar to itself growing at one end only. The length increments are linked to the proportional increase of the radius, preserving the same form throughout the spiral's growth process.

This particular characteristic is attributed to a group of spirals called *logarithmic spirals*. It was first described by **Descartes** (1596-1650) in 1638, and later extensively studied by **Bernoulli** (1654-1705), who was fascinated by the mathematical beauty of this curve and called it the *spira mirabilis (the marvellous spiral)*.

The spiral is a model of transformation through constantly regulated growth focused on what is called the *still point*. The *still point*, as the balancing factor of a spiral, holds the dynamism of the spiral's energy in an organised manner.

All life is motion. Natural movement is not in straight lines, but in spirals, or in spiralling vortices. Spirals are the actual shape of the fluid energy evolving order from chaos. Victor Schauberger saw them as the natural movements of life, from the structure of galaxies down to the atom. The spiral is the most common vehicle for 'correspondences' – as above, so below.

Alick Bartholomew – Hidden Nature

1.2 – The ways to spiral are many – illustrations by Sándor Kabai[I-1]

1.3 – Energy and Form[I-2]

In the beginning was energy; it is primary – the cause; it creates the form in which it wishes to move; the form is the mirror of the energy – the secondary effect.
– Alick Bartholomew

▶ 1.4 – Generating a *spiral*

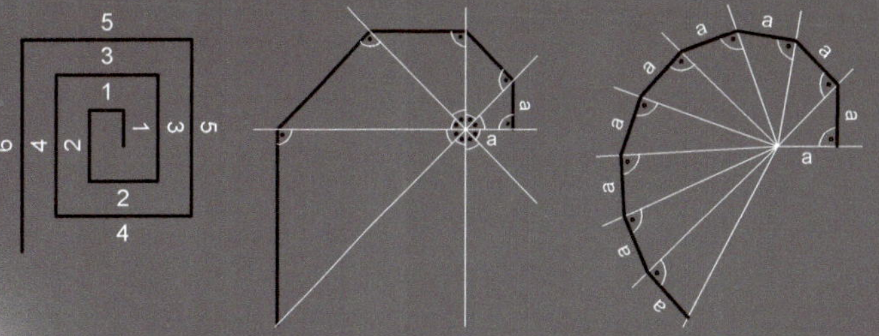

▶ 1.5 – The logarithmic spiral (left) and the Archimedean spiral (right) differentiated by the distance between the spiral arms: in a logarithmic spiral the distance increases in a geometrical progression while in an Archimedean spiral it is constant

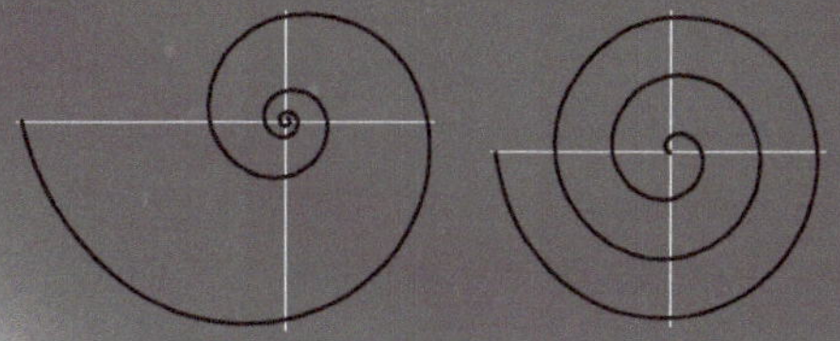

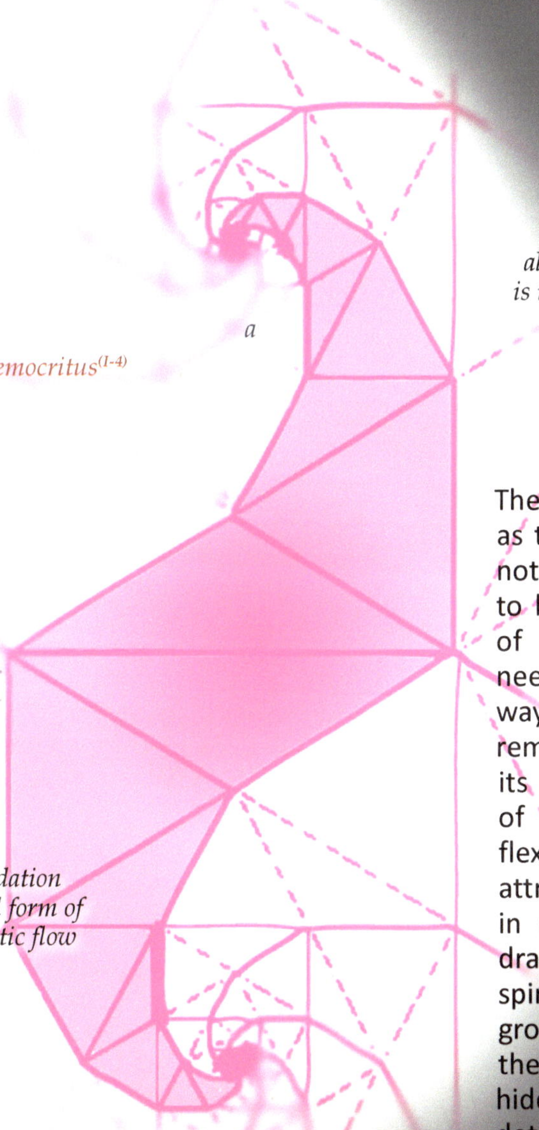

◀ 1.6 – The spidron (a, b), a geometric form made of alternating isosceles triangles, is invented and patented by the Hungarian artist Daniel Erdely [1-3]

In the beginning there was a vortex. – Democritus [1-4]

Matter drawn into Energy wave

Gradual consolidation of outer physical form of the inner energetic flow

PRIMARY ENERGY FLOW

SECONDARY ENERGY FLOW

Physical growth stops where the particles of "frozen" energy are too course to be drawn any further.
The material form is therefore constructed of energetic detritus.

b

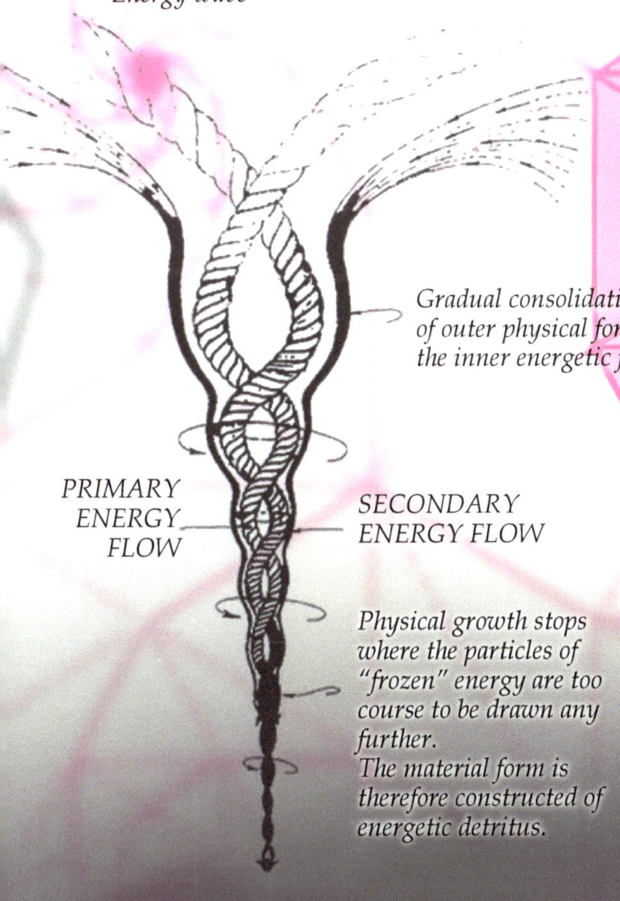

The *still point*, also known as the *eye* of the spiral, is not actually fixed. In order to balance the movement of the spiral's energy, it needs to be flexible. That way the whole system remains stable, preserving its geometry in the face of dynamic growth. This flexibility of the *eye* is an attribute of spirals found in nature, not those we draw on paper. Nature's spirals are alive. They grow and pulsate in the perfection of their hidden mathematical determinant. The spirals drawn on paper are only a record of this life's rhythm.

GOLDEN AND FIBONACCI SPIRALS

The *golden* and *Fibonacci spirals* belong to the *logarithmic spiral* family. Curiously, the circle is a case of a *logarithmic spiral*.

The *golden spiral* can be drawn using the *golden rectangle* (Fig. 1.1) or the *golden triangle* (Fig. 1.9). This spiral is determined by the mathematical constant Φ, that is the *Φ-series*:… 0.618, 1.0; 1.618, 2.618, 4.236, 6.854, 11.090,… *ad infinitum,* while the unfolding of the *Fibonacci spiral* is determined by the *Fibonacci series*: 0, 1, 1, 2, 3, 5, 8, 13, 21, 34, 55, 89, 144,… *ad infinitum*.

The difference between the *Fibonacci* and the *golden spirals* is noticeable in the beginning stage of their unfolding (Fig. 1.10, 1.11).

▼ 1.8 – The golden heart

▼ 1.7 – The harmonic embrace of twelve golden spirals

▲ 1.9 – The birth of the golden spiral within a golden triangle

The golden Mean spiral is the only angle at which a wave can enter itself without hurting itself. This is called SELF-RE-ENTRY. The ability to re-enter self for a wave is called SELF-REFERENCE which simply means the ability to REFER TO YOURSELF. The ability to SELF-REFER is definition of consciousness (The Vedas). This is why the Golden Mean spiral base for waves compressing is the origin of CONSCIOUSNESS (self-reference) and the origin of CREATION PRINCIPLE (perfect way to COMPRESS charge waves).

Daniel Winter[1-5]

The GOLDEN MEAN SPIRAL is Self-Similarity Perfected For Wave Mechanics.

Daniel Winter

> The golden spiral has no beginning and no end. Accordingly, any graphical representation of the golden spiral is just a partial record of its endless route – the one we can perceive while it passes through our dimension.

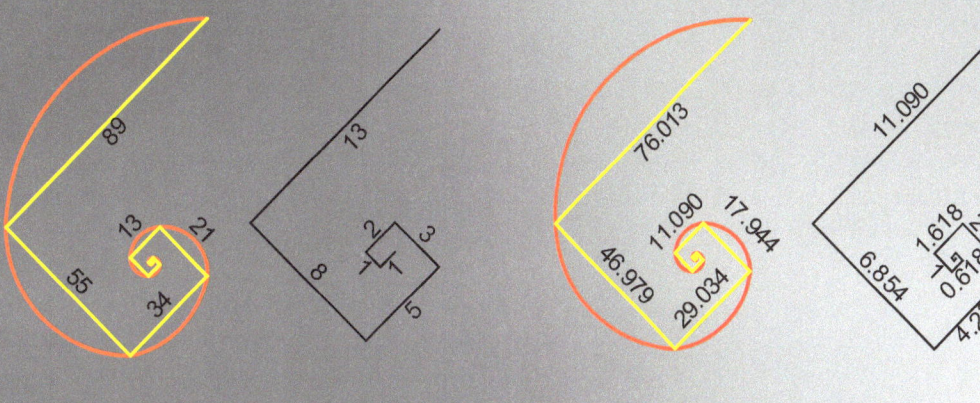

▲ 1.10 – The Fibonacci spiral

▲ 1.11 – The golden spiral

The origin of the *Fibonacci spiral* is Zero (0) and from there it grows only in one direction – outwardly. In the *Fibonacci series,* the ratio between the two consecutive numbers only approximates Φ. This reflects on the form of the *Fibonacci spiral* as an 'imperfection', in comparison to the immaculate *golden spiral* which all along develops through the constant Φ.

Without a beginning and without an end, perfectly following the rhythm of the *golden number,* the *golden spiral* evolves in two directions: inwardly and outwardly. The *still point,* called the *asymptote,* is a symbol of its eternal longing for self-realisation – something we can only witness in the inner dimensions of our being. The *golden spiral* is the Creator's immaculate model of an eternally regulated growth. The *Fibonacci spiral* seems to be its tangible representative, a vehicle through which the *golden spiral* operates in the density of matter.

The *logarithmic spirals* present in nature express a certain rhythm of life and their geometry is a formula of a steady harmony for a growing form.

SPIRALS IN THE PLANT WORLD

The growth of both the *Fibonacci* and the *golden spiral,* as *logarithmic spirals,* is characterised by their transferring of accumulated values of past experiences and building them into the newness of the continuously evolving self. The past is therefore recorded in a form. Every present moment utilises it as a building material and support for the future. Nothing comes out of nothing, and throughout nature *logarithmic spirals* nicely illustrate this life principle.

The *logarithmic spiral's* segments are self-similar in shape, though not the same in actual size. Since the spiral opens wider from the *still point* of its eye, segments grow in size but maintain the same curvature throughout the spiral's body. This particular property is of great significance to biological forms. For example, it is the key behind the stability of a tree. A tree trunk, being a *still point,* balances the ever increasing number of the branches and leaves which follow particular spiral energy lines.

Many plants utilise spiral geometry as a guideline for the development of their parts or the overall form. For example, the leaf endings of some *ferns* curve into spirals which inspired the 17th century Italian craftsmen **Albani** to carve violin heads in that manner.

We can notice spirals in the way the climbers grow up in our garden, as well as in the spiral rosettes of young buds and fully opened blooms of *roses* and *houseleeks*.

▲ 1.12 – Growth marked by spirals

Trees sometimes balance inner and outer forces by twisting their trunks, like the *sweet chestnut* and *beech,* while some African types cover themselves with spikes spirally arranged all along their trunk and branches. Leafy shoots of the *date palm* appear in a spiral system, similar to the way the spikes of some *cacti* are positioned on their body. *Berry fruits,* and elements of the central part of many flowers, are also structured in spiral patterns (Fig. 1.12, 1.15).

The *sunflower head* is a great example of nature's immaculate mathematical skills (Fig. 1.14, 1.15). Florets, that fill the space between the outer petals, mature into seeds arranged into two systems of interlocking left and right spirals. The number of the left and the number of the right spirals are successive *Fibonacci numbers,* or very close to them: usually 34 and 55, although they can be 55 and 89, or even 89 and 144.

The sunflower head also nicely demonstrates the presence of the *golden angle* in nature. That very angle provides the most economical way to utilise space for a constantly growing number of florets. The divergence angle of 137.5°, between successive spirals of florets, can be determined through Φ in the following way:

360/Φ = 360/1.618 = 222.50°
360-222.5 = 137.5°

The *golden angle* can also be observed in the arrangement of leaves, branches and seeds in other plants. In all cases it ensures the highest efficiency in the supply of leaves, branches or seeds, with the nourishment available at a given place. Interestingly, in the world of the tangible, an *irrational number* (Φ) establishes the order of the highest economy and cooperation.

In the geometry of the *conifer cone* and *pineapple,* we also notice spirals as energy lines that rotate in two directions. The points where these energy lines cross, determine the positions of their scales.

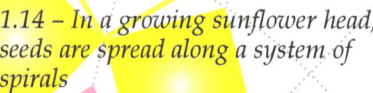

1.14 – In a growing sunflower head, seeds are spread along a system of spirals

◀ *1.15 – Nature avoids the rectilinear and develops its most attractive forms in swelling curves.*
– Joseph Hoffer

The number of spirals in one direction and the number of spirals that wind in the opposite direction, tend to be two consecutive numbers in the *Fibonacci series,* like 8 and 13 or 13 and 21. This way, the spiral growth-forces working through a *conifer cone* and *pineapple* are balanced most efficiently.

PHYLLOTAXIS

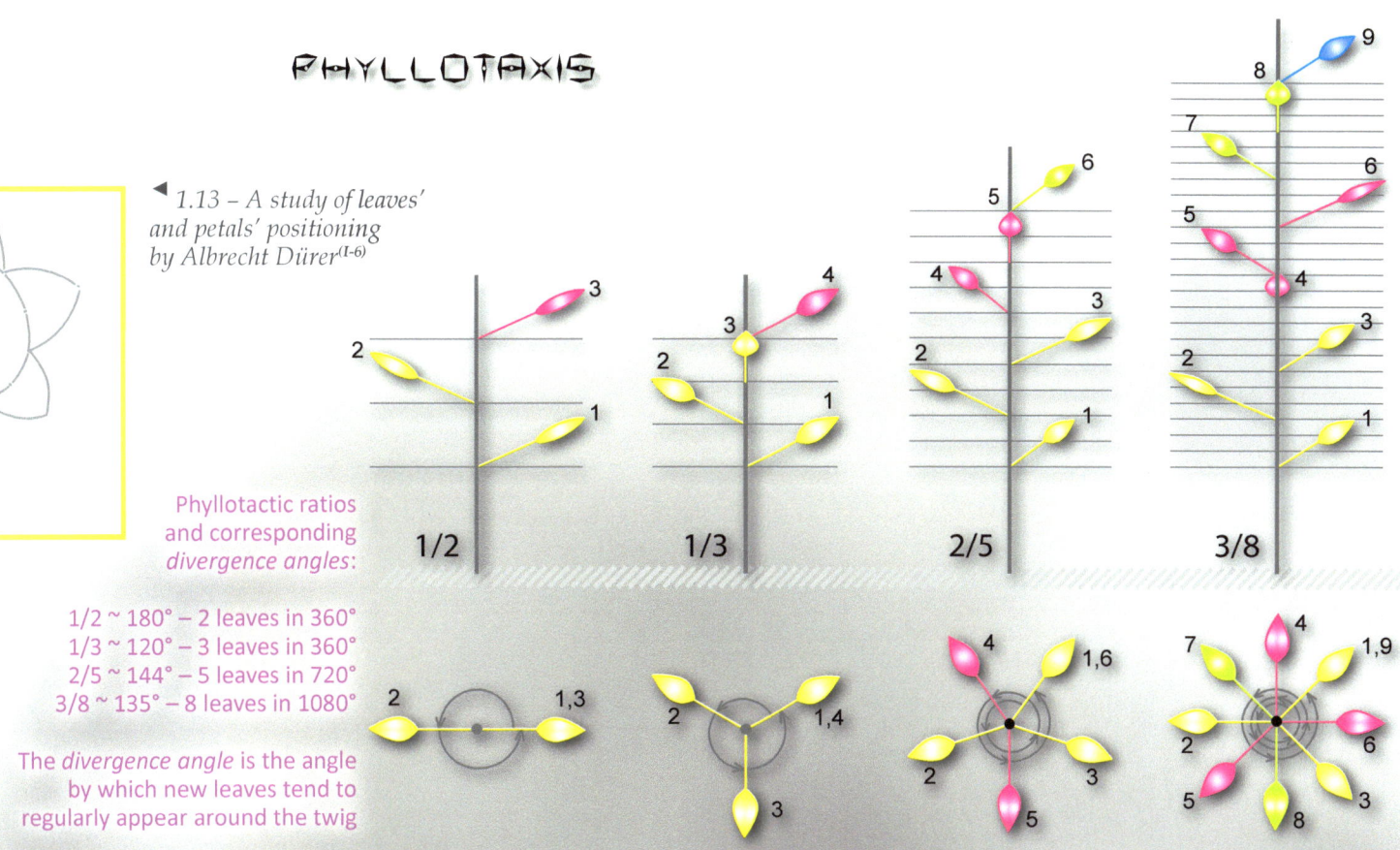

1.13 – A study of leaves' and petals' positioning by Albrecht Dürer[1-6]

Phyllotactic ratios and corresponding *divergence angles*:

1/2 ~ 180° – 2 leaves in 360°
1/3 ~ 120° – 3 leaves in 360°
2/5 ~ 144° – 5 leaves in 720°
3/8 ~ 135° – 8 leaves in 1080°

The *divergence angle* is the angle by which new leaves tend to regularly appear around the twig

1.16 – The arrangement of leaves around a twig is a living diagram of energy motion around the plant

Leaves grow around a twig, or stems along a branch, in the form of a spiral. In 1754, the Swiss naturalist **Charles Bonnet** named the geometrical arrangement of leaves and other plant organs, *phyllotaxis* (from the Greek words *phyllo*=leaf and *taxis*=order). The pattern the leaves adopt optimises their exposure to sun, air and rain, and is expressed by *phyllotactic ratios*: 1/2, 1/3, 2/5 and 3/8. The first figure stands for the number of full 360° rotations it takes for the number of leaves, or stems, specified by the second number to appear. For example, the *phyllotactic ratio* 2/5 means that during two full 360° rotations, five leaves or stems will develop (Fig. 1.16). **Plini**, who lived in the first century BC, noticed the regularity between the appearances of successive leaves, while **Kepler** discovered the presence of the *Fibonacci numbers* in *phyllotactic ratios,* which later became accepted as a general rule.

OTHER LIVING SPIRALS

For much longer than science has kept spirals in its records, some forms in nature have been living through that particular geometry. Around 65 million years ago, *Ammonites*[1-7], a group of marine animals, became extinct leaving their relatives *nautiluses* behind to amaze us with the perfection of their spiral chambers. Fossilised Ammonites reveal the size of the shell to be varying from one inch to nearly nine feet in diameter. What an exhibition of spiral geometry in seawater these moving sculptures were making!

1.17 – *Nature shows us superb examples of organic spirals; the geometry of the human heart* – drawing by **C. W. Leadbeater**

The teeth arrangement in the jaw of the Port Jackson shark, another sea inhabitant, follows a spiral. Elephant's and narwhal's tusks have a spiral curve, while horns of numerous species of *rams* show some of the most peculiar spirals found in the organic world. A ram, for example, has no problem in adjusting its body posture while its horns grow. Since each horn is balanced through the geometry of the spiral and its *still point*, the animal is not bothered with the growth in mass and weight of the horns.

Some other animals utilise spiral geometry though in a different way, like many birds for their flight patterns. Falcons or hawks, storming down towards their prey, through a spiral line maintain an invariable angle of observation. Furthermore, spiral penetration of space encounters less resistance and therefore saves energy. Many insects are also masters of this subtle energy economy and they approach a source of light in a *logarithmic spiral*, which provides them a constant viewing angle as well.

The human embryo, the contractor muscle of our heart, the outer ear, the snail of the interior ear, the fingertips, many seashells, spider webs, tongue of the chameleon, garden snails – all epitomize the *logarithmic spiral* living through biological forms.

BEYOND THE ORGANIC WORLD

Soft lines which suggest the movement of spirals and their intriguing shapes, visible in the plant and animal worlds, have been a constant inspiration to humans. This is illustrated in numerous works of artists and builders starting from Neolithic stones, Etruscan vases, the famous volutes of Greek ionic capitals, to the spiral staircases, columns and even buildings like the Tower of Pisa, the Great Mosque in Samara and the Guggenheim Museum of modern arts in New York.

1.18 – *A spiral happening* – illustration by Sándor Kabai

Bliss – 'the best medicine there is', is scientifically measurable and entrainable. Consciousness' presence and optimal functioning in our body, subjectively perceived as bliss, and now measurable as Internal Cardiac Coherence (ICC) deeply teaches us what health really is.

Frank van den Bovenkamp[1-8]
(Heart Coherence team)

Do not be surprised at Love, do not presume it does not exist. That which introduces You to Yourself is Love. That is the one which makes You Love Yourself. You are a fruit of the Universe which has come into Existence from Seven Shells. It is so difficult to reach You that the first step of this union is Love...

Non-existence means to remain in Your present Consciousness, being unable to Reach Your Own Self. To become an Entity means to discover Your Own Self. If You Discover Yourself, then there is no Non-Existence. Then You can go to wherever You wish, You choose the place You desire. When Your Essence and the Divine Light of Your Spirit Unify, You surpass the Realms.

You are a fruit of Realm, that which will peel Your shell is love. When its magic hand touches You, when You attain the Essence of that vibration, Your sleeping volcano catches fire. Then, there is no more dominance of an influence from the outside to the inside. Your inner volcano melts the shells of Your inner self, one by one, by burning intrinsically.

The Knowledge Book[1-9]
(F24, p 376 par 4; p 377 par 1,2)

The movements of the inner planets, shown dynamically over a period of one full Saturn cycle of 29.46 years, actually describe a vortex, with each planet describing its own spiral path about the Sun. – Alick Bartholomew

▼ 1.19 – The Planetary Vortex
– illustration by Alick Bartholomew[1-2]

That ancient saying: 'What is curved becomes whole' – Are these empty words? To become whole, Turn within.

Lao Tzu[1-10] *(Tao Te Ching)*

▲ 1.20 – Vortex[1-11]

The TURNING INSIDE OUT – Symmetry Skill of SELF RE-ENTRY – Starts AND Steers Tornados. The Universe is MADE of Nothing but Twisters! – Daniel Winter

Equally so, beyond this planet there are many processes, or forms of existence, organised through the geometry of the spiral. Such an example, in our solar system, are Saturn's rings originally spotted by **Galileo Galilei** (1564-1642). According to the latest scientific discoveries they are not separate concentric rings, as it was believed. They are, in fact, formations connected into a spiral wound at least three times around Saturn. Rotating galaxies also generate a spiral appearance, stretching their spiral arms through space. Back on Earth, the rotating motion of storm phenomena like tornadoes or hurricanes is organised in the form of a spiral – just like a body of water swirling down a drain pipe.

SYMBOL OF AN INNER GROWTH

A spiral is an energy line that develops around a *still point* as the best solution to the encountered resistance. Nature's spirals are generated by a constructive interaction of opposing elements. Through its eloquent geometry, the Chinese symbol *Yin-Yang* also suggests a spiral motion as a solution to accumulated dualism.

The grasping of timeless truths and reaching our godly self is a process of a continuous inner transformation. A spiral as a metaphysical category symbolises that journey. With each shift in awareness and each transcended old belief, we come closer to the essence -consciousness of our eternal self.

*There is nothing else
I have ever been
But change.*

*Like a spiral,
Moment to moment,
I grow from the still point
Of Your Love
To Your Consciousness,
My God.*

Milena

Our returning to God is marked by a spiral with no end. The growing of the spiral is a perfect metaphor for the opening and the development of our consciousness while we stay focused on a *still point* within the change. To identify that point, and concentrate on it, is a tremendous evolutionary achievement.

FRACTALS

COMPLEXITY DEFINED	15
DOES THE COASTLINE HAVE AN END	16
SIERPINSKI TRIANGLE	17
DETERMINISTIC METHOD	17
CHAOS GAME	18
MAPPING THE TERRITORY	19
EXAMPLES OF FRACTALS IN NATURE	21
FREE WILL IS RELEVANT TO A GIVEN FRAMEWORK	23
GEOMETRY OF SELF-AWARENESS	24
WHEN WE DWELL IN OUR HEART WE ARE AT ONE WITH EVERYTHING	25
NATURAL GÜRZ CRYSTAL	27

COMPLEXITY DEFINED

In the process of self-expressing, the Creator manifested a very unusual geometry called *fractals*. Fractals are characterised by a potential for an infinite and perfect organising, packing-unpacking, storing and co-existing of the elements in the way that mirrors their whole.

We ought not... to believe that the banks of the ocean are really deformed, because they have not the form of a regular bulwark; nor that the mountains are out of shape, because they are not exact pyramids or cones; nor that the stars are unskilfully placed, because they are not situated at uniform distance... – reflected **Richard Bentley**, the 17th century English scholar.

With this thought in mind, while studying 'formless' forms and the morphology of the 'amorphous', the Polish mathematician **Benoit Mandelbrot** formulated a new geometry of nature in the 1975 naming it *fractal* after the Latin adjective *fractus*, related to the verb *frangere* which means *to break*. This geometry describes many seemingly irregular patterns around us, recognising the rule in the process of fragmenting where each succeeding level is organised in an identical way.

Euclidean geometry, more than 2000 years old, is not suitable to describe fractals. It explains basic geometrical forms the size and scale of which are determined by a whole number – for example, both the sphere and the cube have one cardinal size each, given through r (radius for a sphere) and l (length of a cube's side). Fractals, on the other hand, do not have a specific size and are independent of scale. They repeat a fragment through a simple and perfect rule which enables the structure to grow, so that the initial form evolves through a number of dimensions. The mathematical definition of fractals is a recursive algorithm, unlike the Euclidean forms which are defined by simple algebraic formulae.

The concept of the fractal dimension is very important for understanding the nature of fractals.

There are a few approaches to the notion of the fractal dimension. However, all definitions of fractal dimensions, in their own way, offer a description of how completely a fractal appears to fill space, as one zooms down to finer and finer scales. The most simple is the dimension of similarity. It is used in fractals that exhibit self-similarity wherein the structural complexity of a fractal fragment on all vertical levels is mathematically uniform. During the time when the expression *monster curves* was still used for fractals, in 1919, **Felix Hausdorff** (1868-1942) has offered a definition of their dimension as a non-integer positive real value and significantly contributed to the explanation of elaborate fractal geometry.

Nowadays fractals are a versatile interdisciplinary tool used in mathematics, natural sciences and even art. They are of help to computer designers in the computer and video game industry, in their realistic rendering of natural images in computer graphics, and in the film industry for simulating various environments – since fractal geometry produces convincing results. Fractals were detected even in the behavioural patterns of the stock market, some 70 years ago by the work of **Ralf Nelson Elliott**.

The cell and its Structure which is the Soul of You, My Human Beings, and the infinite rotations within My Cosmos, which are My Soul, are the SAME. The System directing the Feelings in You, My Cosmos and the Electro Magnetic Waves and frequencies providing the OMNIPOTENCE in Me are the SAME. The Ability and Creativity in You, My Human Beings, and the Nucleus which is My ESSENCE are the SAME.

Great Power
The Knowledge Book (F40, p 674, par 3)

DOES THE COASTLINE HAVE AN END

Holistic or spiritual science sees Nature as a mirror of the original creative impulse in the Universe, a manifestation of the Universal Mind, or The-All-That-Is.

Alick Bartholomew (Hidden Nature)

Fractals are self-organising structures. Their form may only appear non-orderly but in reality it is a complex geometric pattern. That complexity is most often organised through the principle of self-similarity, though not every fractal follows it.

The Cosmic Fractal, Icosa-Dodeca perfect stellation, perfectly matches the ratio of self-similarity of the Mandelbrot fractal...

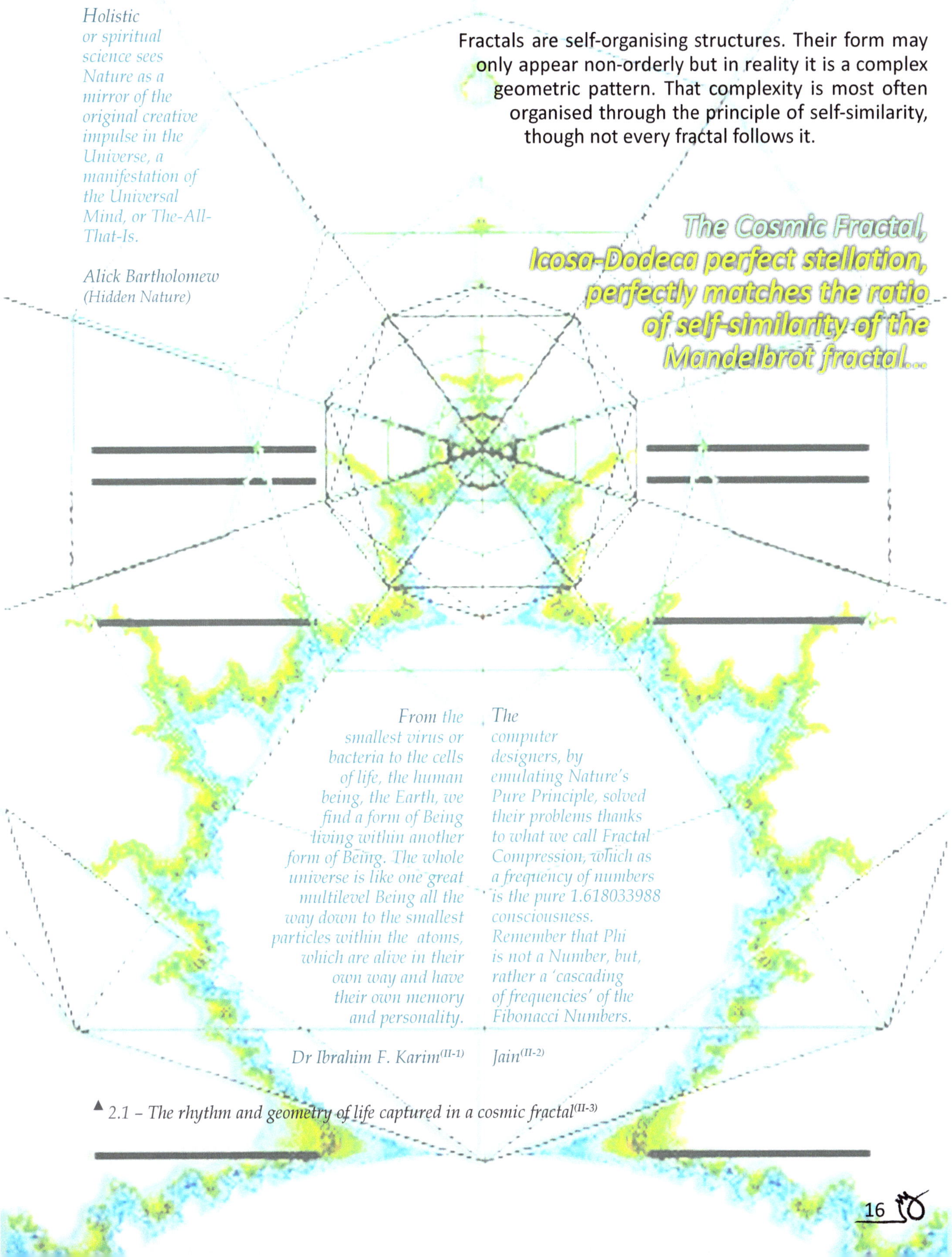

From the smallest virus or bacteria to the cells of life, the human being, the Earth, we find a form of Being living within another form of Being. The whole universe is like one great multilevel Being all the way down to the smallest particles within the atoms, which are alive in their own way and have their own memory and personality.

Dr Ibrahim F. Karim[II-1]

The computer designers, by emulating Nature's Pure Principle, solved their problems thanks to what we call Fractal Compression, which as a frequency of numbers is the pure 1.618033988 consciousness. Remember that Phi is not a Number, but, rather a 'cascading of frequencies' of the Fibonacci Numbers.

Jain[II-2]

▲ 2.1 – The rhythm and geometry of life captured in a cosmic fractal[II-3]

A coastline is a good example of a fractal with no inherent self-similarity. Coastlines also very nicely illustrate the transcendental nature of fractals.

If we analyse the coastline of any island intending to measure its length as precisely as we can, this is what is going to happen. The precision of our results will differ in accordance with the accuracy of the tool we use for measuring. Using shorter and shorter rulers, we will be able to be more and more precise by going around smaller and smaller fragments of the coastline, as if straightening it with each step. When we are to measure every bit of these fragments, in lengths smaller than one centimetre, then smaller, and yet smaller…, it will seem as if we were endlessly extending the length of the coastline by ultimately stretching it to form a circle. For every new level of detail, there is another more detailed level that explains it, and so on (Fig. 2.2). This phenomenon is a fractal. Its leitmotif in theory can endlessly repeat itself within a finite space – hence the transcendental property of fractal geometry.

SIERPINSKI TRIANGLE

The construction of fractals can be shown in the example of the *Sierpinski triangle* (Fig. 2.3) which is an easily understandable fractal form. The Polish mathematician **Waclaw Sierpinski** (1882-1969) demonstrated it in 1915 by cutting out the triangle formed by the midpoints of each side of the initial triangle and repeating the same process upon each new triangle (in the figure 2.3 the white triangles have been cut out).

The following two ways of getting to the *Sierpinski triangle* illustrate two opposing methods called the *deterministic* and the *chaos game*.

DETERMINISTIC METHOD

We start by determining the midpoints of each side of an equilateral triangle as the vertices of a new smaller central triangle. Then we colour it (white), or cut it out as **Sierpinski** did. The same procedure is repeated on every new generation of triangles. Triangles obtained this way have sides exactly one-half of the original triangle and an area exactly one-quarter of the original triangle's area. Also, each new triangle is similar to the original one. Iterating this process produces more and more new, and smaller, triangles indrawn into the latest generation. Each generation maintains self-similarity with each level and with the initial triangle.
In the geometry of fractals, the number of constructing steps/levels/generations of fragments is potentially infinite. Fractal structures can vary in size, but the pattern of organisation remains the same on all levels.

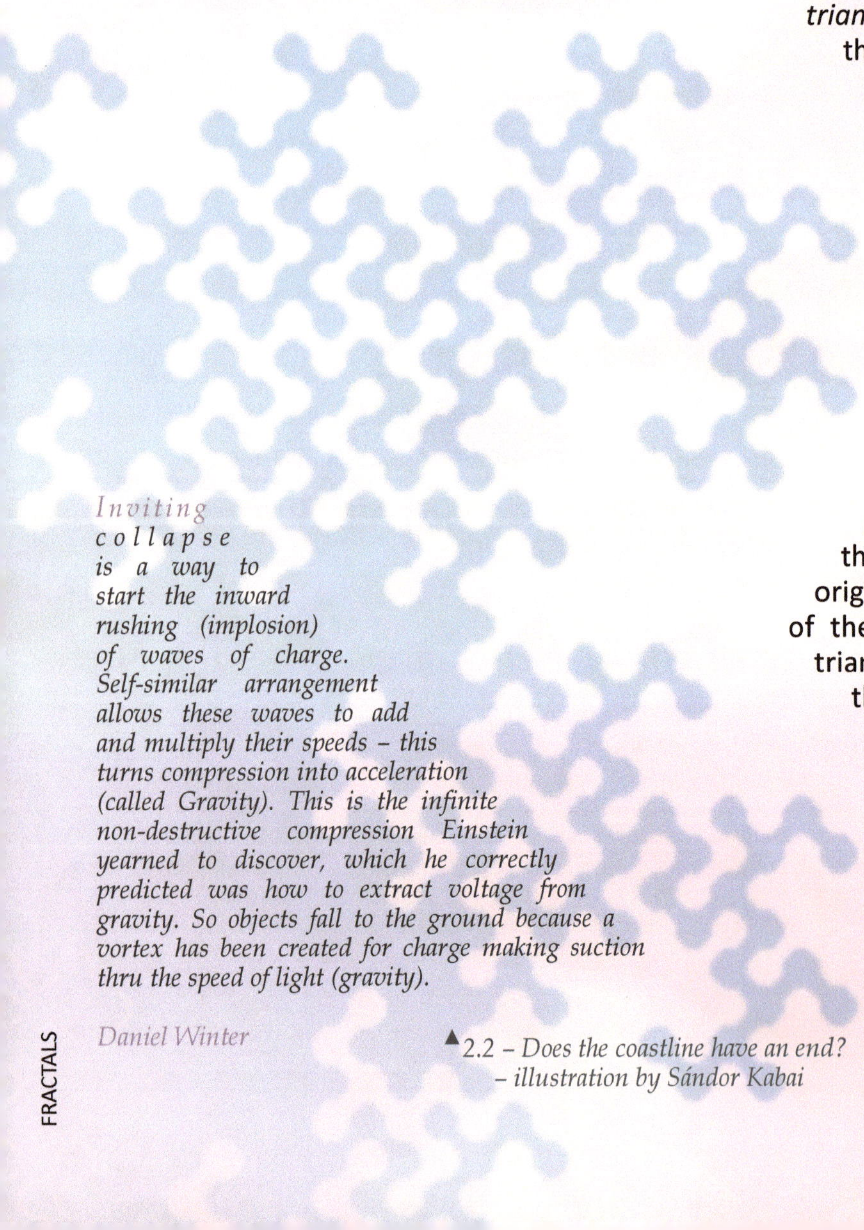

Inviting collapse is a way to start the inward rushing (implosion) of waves of charge. Self-similar arrangement allows these waves to add and multiply their speeds – this turns compression into acceleration (called Gravity). This is the infinite non-destructive compression Einstein yearned to discover, which he correctly predicted was how to extract voltage from gravity. So objects fall to the ground because a vortex has been created for charge making suction thru the speed of light (gravity).

Daniel Winter

▲ 2.2 – *Does the coastline have an end? – illustration by Sándor Kabai*

▲ *2.3 – Sierpinski triangle – the same essence propagated through a potentially infinite number of levels*

CHAOS GAME

Another way of arriving at the fractal geometry of a *Sierpinski triangle* can be demonstrated through a *chaos game* performed on an equilateral triangle[II-4]. The game starts by colouring three vertices of a triangle in three different colours. Here, we will use *red, blue* and *green*. Then, we need a die with two sides red, two blue and two green. Afterwards, we take any spot inside the triangle as a starting position of what is called the *seed point*.

The game is played by rolling the die to get a colour and then moving the *seed point* half the distance to the vertex of that colour (Fig. 2.4a). Every new position of the *seed point* is the beginning point of the next step. The colour the die shows always indicates the next colour vertex we will move the *seed point* to. After a few (five or six) rolls, we can start recording the position of the *seed point*'s movements. To obtain visible results, the procedure should include a few hundred steps more, though the rolling of the die could go on *ad infinitum*.

To explain the geometry of the *seed point*'s movement, we will use the triangle ABC shown in figure 2.4b.

The *seed point* is initially positioned as the centroid of the triangle $A_1B_1C_1$ (ABC). From there, in the first step, the *seed point* hops onto the centroid of one of three next smaller triangles in the direction of the vertex – the colour of which is revealed by the rolling die. Since it always chooses the place that is half-way between one of the vertices of the initial triangle ABC and its own actual position, according to the geometry of the equilateral triangle the *seed point* continuously moves into the centroid of only one triangle from the next-smaller generation of triangles. At some stage of the game, the *seed point* is actually ready to hop into an invisibly small triangle.

At first glance, and to the untrained eye, this game does not promise any order. It looks like a perfect path to meaningless chaos and its result is like a smear image of a never-ending trajectory. How many times would what we call *chance* turn out not to be so? There is depth, order and meaning in everything. Whether we perceive it or not, depends on the context in which we make our observation.

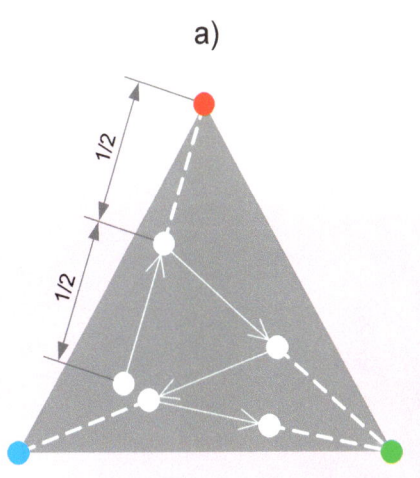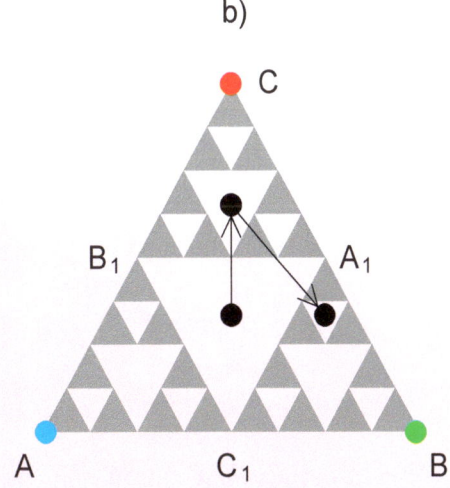

◀ *2.4 – Constructing the Sierpinski triangle by chaos game method illustrates that chaos is governed by invisible forces of order*

However chaotic certain discordant environments and phenomena may appear to be, within a wider picture they are nothing but a playing field for the creative forces of order. The ordering tendency of these forces is often concealed behind the plurality of relationships, movements and possibilities. Our personal chaotic states, for example, have an important role in opening us towards the unexpected. They actually offer surprisingly suitable choices and test our ability to focus at the same time.

So, what does this hopping *seed point,* mapped by each move, determine with the rolling of the die? The result of all of its positions is a dotted pattern which eventually reveals the *Sierpinski triangle*. Interestingly, if the *seed point* starts this journey even outside the initial triangle, by hopping according to the rules of the chaos game, it will describe the *Sierpinski triangle* within that initial triangle.

The seemingly chaotic abstract paintings of American artist **Jackson Pollock** (1912-1956), contain an order beyond our perception. A computer analysis of his paintings has revealed fractal geometry behind impulsive colour lines thus adding to our understanding of chaos (order).

MAPPING THE TERRITORY

As we could notice in the example of the *Sierpinski triangle* drawn by the method of the *chaos game*, even so-called *chaos* is ruled by forces of order. Often, to recognise that order is quite a task.

▲ *2.5 – The Sierpinski triangles joined into a new pattern*

In Mathematical terms, Embedding IS How to become ONE with Anything! Embedding IS How A Wave Survives by Branching Non-Destructively Into A PHractal.
– Daniel Winter

While searching for order within seemingly unconnected events and circumstances, we gradually acquire an understanding of the reasons and principles that guide the ongoing processes, on a personal as well as on a general level. With every situation we go through, a dot on the territory of emerging patterns is defined – just as casting a die determines the direction of the next step in the *chaos game*. Each dot counts and gets us closer to seeing the regularity. When the existence of a pattern enters our awareness, we attain a new level of understanding, we see the bigger picture and life continues from a higher level. A fresh attitude is gained through every realised cause and effect.

Would it not be interesting to see the resulting pattern of our entire life's journey? If we are consistently focused on the three principles, at some level of that pattern, is the *Sierpinski triangle* going to appear? Whatever happens, the pattern that we are completing is the one known as a life programme or destiny. In the cosmic archives, it is stored as our personal life-mandala. Before entering an incarnation, WE also are involved in producing its design and that is one of the reasons we cannot escape anything that is in our destiny. However, in this world of the physical, our mandala is our own puzzle. With each new experience we identify its new dots to make it come alive.

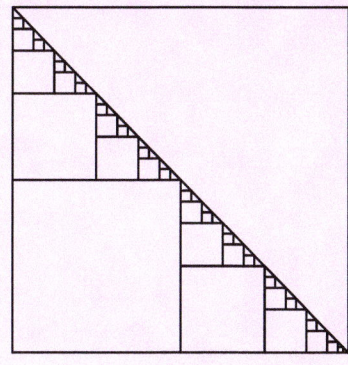 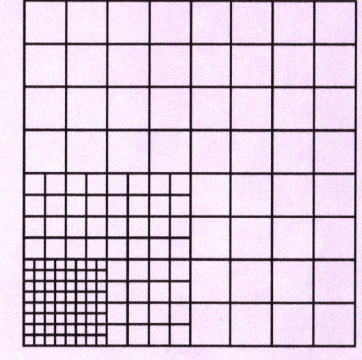

▲ 827 – The square, exploring itself through fractal geometry

*I Am That I Am and you are My expression.
You are the living whole – that through which I see Myself.
And just as well, so it is with you that every blade of grass,
every natural form of life, is an expression for you
of another part of your Real self.*

The Messages from God[(II-5)]
through Yael and Doug Powell

Organic growth and development require harmony. Resonance is the process by which harmony is brought to lower systems which than provide a firm basis upon which higher structures may be built.

Alick Bartholomew
(Hidden Nature)

◄ 2.6 – Dürer's fractal snowflake

2.8 – *A Romanesco cauliflower – an immaculate model of the self-propagated form*

And when you have reached the mountaintop, then you shall begin to climb.

Kahlil Gibran

EXAMPLE OF FRACTALS IN NATURE

Nature exhibits diversity not only on a horizontal plane but also in a multilevel complexity. The organisation of these levels of complexity, in some natural structures, is now better understood and easier explained through the concept of fractals. For example, **Daniel Winter** sees fractals as a perfect example of the way nature compresses life-force and to him fractality means *harmonic inclusiveness*.

The natural sciences like physics, biology, chemistry, meteorology, seismology, medicine, soil mechanics, geology, in their own domains, find the fractal geometry particularly suitable for explaining seemingly irregular shapes and processes.

The scientific community has developed the so-called *fractal analysis*. It is a method of modelling data by applying the fractal characteristics to sound, light, images, objects or phenomena. Thus biologists study the diffusion of complex proteins, the human brain surface, and the branching of some inner system of the human body like the lungs, or classify animals with the use of fractals. Materials sciences find fractals to be a valuable guide for analysing surface structures while those who wander into the microscopic level of condensed matter witness the intricate geometry of fractals organising even the tiniest particles. In areas like vibrations and music, fractals also provide explanations of many phenomena.

2.9 – *Nature is an open gallery of growing shapes, wherein the principle of self-similarity is employed to perfection*

In cosmology, for example, since ancient times, well before fractals were defined as a mathematical notion, there have been some views that assumed a hierarchical and fractal-like structure of the universe. Some recent minor cosmology theories assign fractal properties to the distribution of matter and galaxies within the universe, as well as to the way a universe sprouts self-similar new universes.

The common findings of all these scientists are of forms structured by self-similar portions through different levels. In other words, they witness the whole endeavouring to infinitely multiply its own self-similar fragments, which are wholes in their own right, and how the wholeness of a natural entity is bigger than the sum of its parts.

The popularity of these geometrical forms in the realm of nature is becoming increasingly evident. Some of our inner organs, many outer shapes, movements and phenomena, are structured through fractals, and the list seems to be endless: *pituitary glands, roses, onions, ferns, geological topography, ecosystem boundaries, ocean waves, clouds, rain, lightning, river systems, mountain profiles; the movement of flame, smoke,* and *fluids; seismic faults,* and even *galaxy clusters* (Fig. 2.8, 2.9, 2.10).

Fractals provide a wave 'message' path for form, shape, and vibration into higher and higher evolving patterns – an encoded thread linking larger spirals into smaller spirals and on to infinity.

Daniel Winter

Energy, woven into FRACTALITY like a rose, concentrates LIFE FORCE and lights your DNA into only sustainable – real inner fire!

Daniel Winter

All of biology uses fractal principle to attract the charge field (spirit/chi/orgone/barraka/shakti) into perfect compression called LIFE.

Daniel Winter

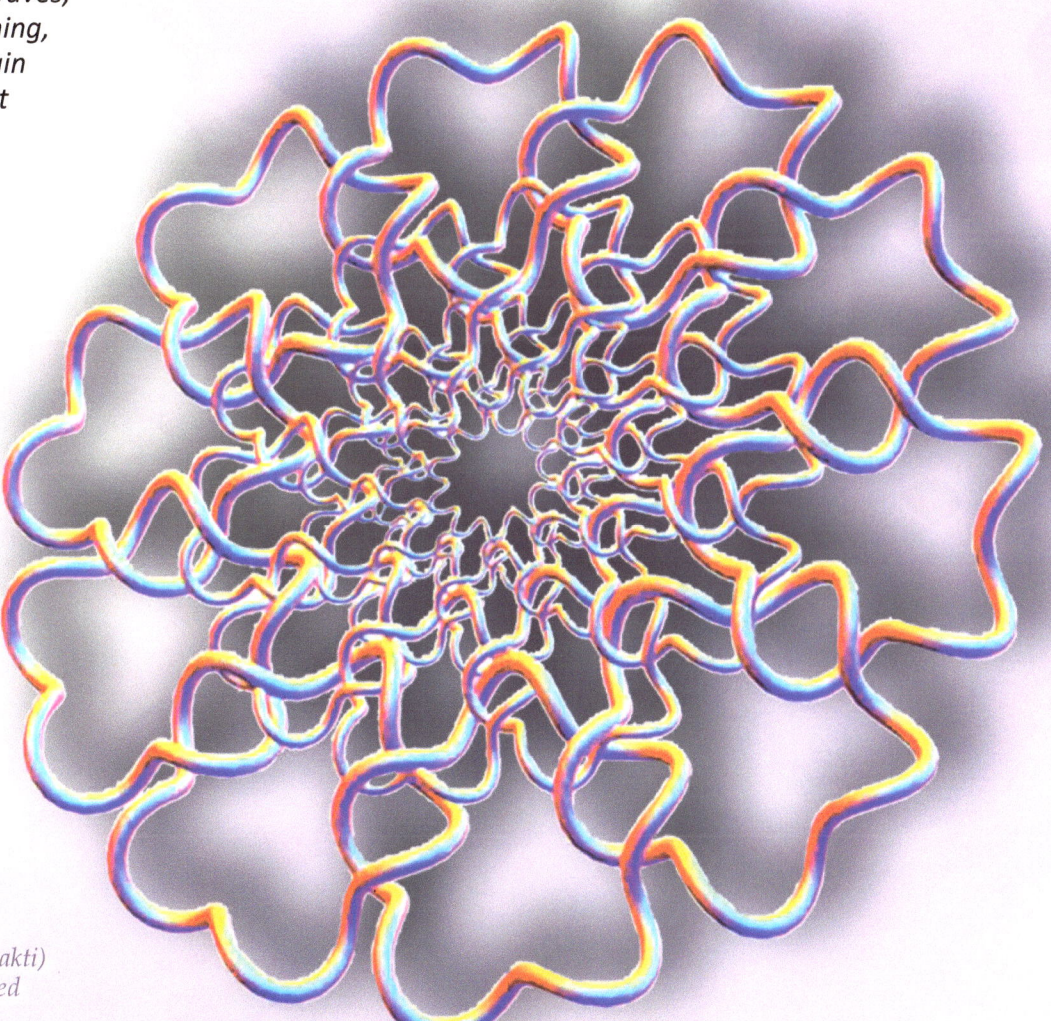

▲ 2.10 – *Wave on a wave, waving as a fractal flower* – illustration by Sándor Kabai

A tree branches through an iteration of fractal segments so that its branches achieve maximum exposure with minimum interference (Fig. 2.11). This geometrical principle, present in plant morphogenesis, is called *phyllotaxis*[II-6] and is often based on the *golden proportion*. It represents the wisdom of nature on how to use and share space to the utmost benefit of all concerned.

The *golden proportion's* property, of dividing while maintaining a connection to the whole, secures a coherent fragmentation, unpacking and organisation of an infinite scope. In a plant's life, the application of this principle enables the most effective supply of the branches' endpoints with the nourishment from the soil and light from the Sun. However, in case of a river system, or capillaries in human organs, like alveoli in the lungs, we can observe growth of a branching system that does not comply with the self-similarity rule.

The tree branching examples, featured in figures 2.11, 2.13 and 2.14, differ only in the angle in which the repeated fragment appears.

FREE WILL IS RELEVANT TO A GIVEN FRAMEWORK

Although fractal levels are predictable, in nature these levels can exhibit a certain casualness as a result of environmental factors or of free will (choice). However, free will is only relevant to a given framework. For example, every branch of a tree will have some individuality, in the way it develops within its own fractal segment, but will inevitable comply with the fractal structuring within the crown.

▼ 2.11 – *Fractal branching – the way the intelligence of a tree works on modelling its own physical form*

Consciousness has an inherent spectrum of frequencies – as does anything – and can duplicate energies it detects/receives by resonance. It becomes the same wavelength as the source, bringing about instantaneous transmission of information.

Dr Noel Huntley[II-7]

When you choose to feel compassion – you make a little picture INSIDE your heart – which WHEN it is SELF-SIMILAR (or fractal) to the SHAPE of the FEELING (magnetism) of the person OUTSIDE your heart… THEN that sets up the conditions to allow the OUTSIDE to FALL IN. This is called technically – a FRACTAL ATTRACTOR. It works because only FRACTAL (or self-similar, fern or onion like) symmetry permits infinite non-destructive compression. This is also called IMPLOSION.

Daniel Winter

When the harmonics of the brain-body-heart-planet enter into NESTING they do it by the principle of FRACTALITY. The small is within the large; the pattern in the wave core of hydrogen is the same shaped slip knot which makes your heart muscle – and is the same as the HEART of the SUN.

Daniel Winter

The ultimate and most simple definition of the Golden mean is one word: SHARING.

Jain

GEOMETRY OF SELF-AWARENESS

Beyondness dwells within. The Creator equipped us with the ability to contemplate solar systems, or look at the landscape around us, and perceive the vastness of these phenomena with tiny brain cells. These cells host our cerebral consciousness. They reach and process the energies of higher worlds, while our body operates within the energy/evolutionary dimension of Mother Earth.

Fractals are the Creator's divine ladders for vertical organisation of His own fragments in a most harmonious way. By establishing an order even within seemingly chaotic areas, through this geometry, the Creator enables a continuous evolvement according to the rules of that order.

The pentagonal drawing in figure 2.12 can serve as a geometrical model of self-awareness (self-referencing) and sustainable growth. It can also illustrate the mechanism behind spiritual self-regeneration in a harmonious manner. Pentagrams, inscribed in pentagons, in their central parts define a new generation of pentagons. These new pentagons, like the new cells of an organism, enlarge the charge capacity of the whole and provide a ground for the repetition of the process on a new level.

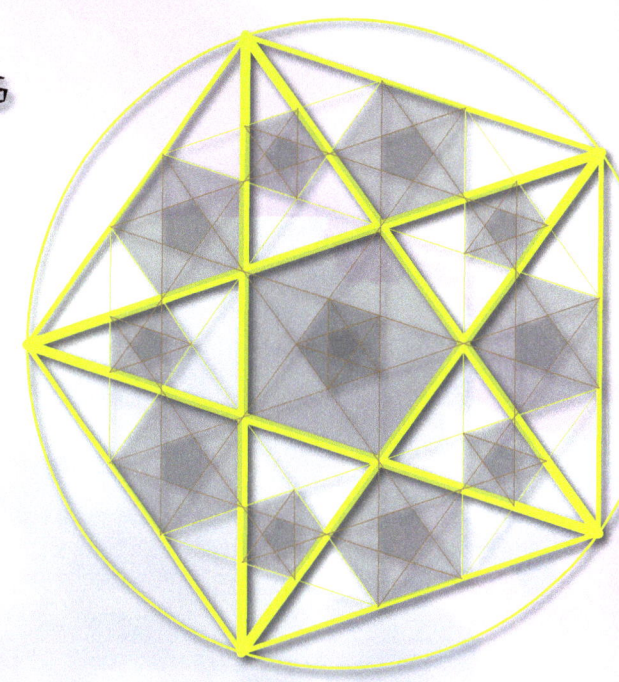

▲ 2.12 – A Φ-based fractal – When the outside falls inside, in a fractal way, the outside/inside symmetry of information is infinitely provided

Bliss is the condition of ability to radiate charge to infinity sustainable. This requires perfect fractal embedding. It is also the (self-referent) definition of how electrical fields become self organizing and self aware.

Daniel Winter

▼ 2.13 – *The self-similarity of the inside to the outside predicts the amount of gravity created by atom, DNA, plants and stars.*
– Daniel Winter

▶ 2.14 – Tree branching examples differ only in the angle which branches take

Self-similarity electrically attracts charge, and therefore Life, because self-similarity attracts non-destructive compression.

Daniel Winter

Depending on which direction we choose to follow in this kind of geometry, it can endlessly lead us inwards (through diminution) or outwards (through augmentation). Fractals are a suitable illustration of multidimensionality.

Fractals based on the regular pentagon and pentagram, are instructional templates for an immaculate compression/expansion-like organisation of waves through the *golden proportion* (Fig. 1.9). Both the pentagon and the pentagram are made of *golden triangles,* meaning that the *golden spirals* can whirl through them and reinforce their energy fields.

Φ is a ratio that teaches the parts to agree, and harmoniously join to last together on the road with no end. Thus the concordance, based on the *golden proportion,* is a sure ticket to eternity.

WHEN WE DWELL IN OUR HEART, WE ARE AT ONE WITH EVERYTHING

Within the fractal of *All That Is,* we are fragments created with the idea to reflect the Divine on our own dimensional level.

The beauty outside of us, like the beauty of a butterfly, a mountain, a or a tree, can trigger the Divine in us.

Field effect called FEELING –
is the ability to feel charge and magnetism:
'The Wind Upon Which Love Travels'.

Daniel Winter

Life IS THE PROCESS of getting organic molecules fractally enough arranged to compress CHARGE…

DNA can only feed and grow in the environment of fractal capacitive charge. Biology builds these fields to initiate the fractal charge distribution which animates the centre of all life…

Nature was built to teach you precisely this – get FRACTAL or get DEAD, and was built to deliver PERMANENT DEATH quickly to all those who refuse to learn.

Daniel Winter

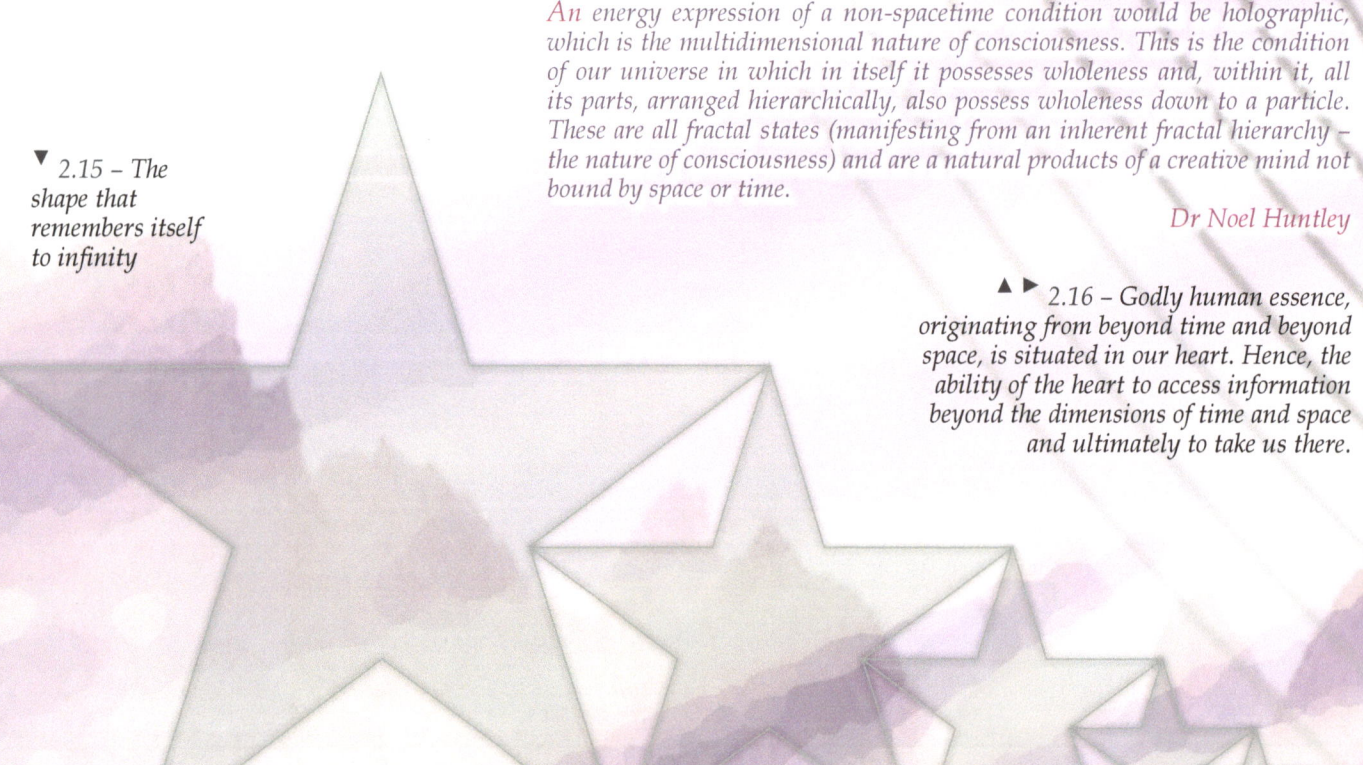

▼ 2.15 – The shape that remembers itself to infinity

An energy expression of a non-spacetime condition would be holographic, which is the multidimensional nature of consciousness. This is the condition of our universe in which in itself it possesses wholeness and, within it, all its parts, arranged hierarchically, also possess wholeness down to a particle. These are all fractal states (manifesting from an inherent fractal hierarchy – the nature of consciousness) and are a natural products of a creative mind not bound by space or time.

Dr Noel Huntley

▲ ▶ *2.16 – Godly human essence, originating from beyond time and beyond space, is situated in our heart. Hence, the ability of the heart to access information beyond the dimensions of time and space and ultimately to take us there.*

The holy GRAIL is in your Heart when you chose perfect fractal and very attractive perfect compression that is LOVE itself.

Daniel Winter

▸ 2.17 – The spidron – illustration by Daniel Erdely and Rinus Roelofs

Your planet is addicted to states of pain and grief and sorrow. Your news services are filled with disaster and death, and so you confuse emotional responses of pity and fellow-feeling with Compassion.

Dearest ones, understand that Compassion is Spiritual Service: to find Joy and Peace within yourself and to pass it on to others. This means that you will need to release addictions to disasters and suffering and dramas of pain. Do not create them in your own lives and do not support them in the lives of others. Rather – focus your Compassionate Hearts on bringing positive energies and love, and the Message of Hope and Unity to all those you meet.
This is Compassion!

The New Earth will be based on the understanding of Compassion. On living this truth – that only Love is real and that only Love and Sharing are true and valid experiences.

Lady Quan Yin
through
Celia Fenn[II-8]

We are also capable of finding God inside of us, consciously, like in the serenity of our heart. Both of these roads lead to the blissful state of being – which is what ultimately the absolute singularity is. Thus, rolling down the fractal levels, whenever we experience beauty and bliss in our heart, the Divine echoes through us.

Fractals provide a suitable model of coherence and endless interconnectedness within the Total. When we hold an awareness of God, His fractal touch becomes real to us. It opens us towards a more intensive experience of the godly presence, of our own self.

Similarly, belonging to any social organisation, exposes us to an additional supply of life-force that flows through it. That is a reward for those who know how to harmoniously share their own is-ness within the diversity of views. Becoming fractal secures a lasting and fruitful coexistence.

The human heart is nested in the heart of God. The centre of our supreme power is therefore in our heart and love is a major tool for reaching it.

Love is also an evolutionary catalyst and the evolvement path of our consciousness. From the experience of love as an emotion, translated from the thought frequency of a *terrestrial consciousness*, across spiritual love, we arrive at love as a divine vibration independent of emotions. After we learn to liberate ourselves from emotional suffering incurred by our thoughts, we love consciously, unendingly, and without discrimination: plants, animals, humans, indeed the whole Creation. By reaching this consciousness we are on the way to becoming the owners of our spiritual energy, to fully integrate with our own godly essence. The human being on this level of consciousness/love helps others to climb their evolutionary stairs by projecting his/her embracing energy onto the environment.

When we dwell in our heart, we are at one with everything and feel no boundaries between the inside and the outside. The ability to mirror the outer world in our heart and feel it inside, **Daniel Winter** calls *compassion*.

All That Is perpetually maintains the flow of information and life throughout its complex body. Since each one of us is a part of the grand fractal of Creation, each one of us is also omnipresent by living through our own numerous replicas on other levels. That is why it is not surprising that each one of our 64 billion evolutionary completed cells can be used to produce our duplicate. The cell is a fractal unit of godly potential in the material realms. It originates from *mud-water-cosmic beams* synthesis. The single cell is a holder of the most compressed energy/information charge acquired over the unknown depths of time[II-9].

Fractals – what a way to spread awareness and organise life-force while preserving the memory of the origin, of the Creator!

NATURAL GÜRZ CRYSTAL

Natural Gürz crystal (Fig. 2.18), as well as its 1800 *mini atomic wholes* composed of *universes, cosmoses, realms* and *galactic clusters*[II-10], is depicted through the Greek letter *alpha*. Besides the congruent shapes and the structure, the operational ordinance of the *Gürz crystal* and the *mini atomic wholes* are also equivalent. Many similarities between the macro and micro levels illustrate the fractal nature of this mega cosmic organism, introduced to our planet with *The Knowledge Book*.

The *Gürz crystal*, or *atomic whole*, which floats on the *Thought Ocean of the Pre-Eminent Power*, has three distinctive natural parts as three natural dimensions:

1. The **Dimension of NOTHINGNESS** (the *Dimension of Absolute Time* where there is no evolution, no incarnation; no energy as we know it – only BREATH.) This is the *Dimension of the* **ALMIGHTY** where His unchanging Laws and Ordinances rule.

2. The **Dimension of LIFE** is also called the *Main Existential dimension, Mighty Energy Focal Point, Biological Universe, Second Universe* and the *Dimension of Adam and Eve*. This is a dimension where spiral vibrations supervise the energies emanated from the *Infinite Positive* and the *Infinite Negative Universes* and hold them together. The togetherness of the energies from these two opposite universes is crucial for the formation of the *atomic whole* itself. The *Main Existential dimension* is a dimension of authority pertaining to the act of bringing into existence. Those in charge of the *Main Existential dimension* are three equivalent energy totalities called the **Pre-Eminent Spirit**, the **Pre-Eminent Mother** and the **Creator**. In cooperation with the *Lordly mechanism* that prepares the single biological cell, the **Pre-Eminent Mother** here connects the spiritual energy to that cell while the **Creator** unifies His essence-energy with it thus creating the *soul seed*. In order to complete its evolution, the *soul seed* is then transferred by the *Technological dimension* to the evolvement medium of the most suitable existential dimensions of the *mini atomic wholes* within the *Dimension of Allness*.

3. The **Dimension of ALLNESS** (*Dimension of the* **ALL-DOMINATING** – *Dimension of Evolution* – *Dimension of Space and Time*)

In the book *All is Number*, section on the number *Seven*, we got to know the geometry behind the pyramidal mechanism within the *Light-Universe* that collects the Energy of the *Thought Ocean of the Pre-Eminent Power* and projects it onto the *Main Existential dimension* from where it is directed to the *Reality of the Unified Humanity* (Fig.2.19). All that energy received, the *Reality of the Unified Humanity* distributes within the *atomic whole* to feed each *soul seed/life seed* with the Thought Power arrived from the *Thought Universe*. This chain of reflections supplies the different energy levels of the *Dimension of Allness* with the essence of life, thus propagating the knowledge and evolvement parallel to the law of equilibrium.

Besides the single *natural Gürz crystal*, there are millions of artificial *Gürz crystals* floating on the *Thought Ocean*. All of them are the *Gürz crystals* of the *alpha* generation and are connected like balloons with strong energy ropes, the same as *mini atomic wholes* are connected within each *Gürz crystal*. The totality in which all *atomic wholes* exist, that is, all *Gürzes* exist, is called the *MAIN atomic whole* or *Thought Universe* and this totality is placed within the *GREAT atomic whole* or the *Consciousness Ocean*.

Thus every location in the universe is unique. Its address is the informational frequency at its manifestation (say, our environment). Its going inwards nonlinearly into higher dimensions, in a state of resonance with greater inner-frequencies, unites to the whole. For example, an atom will be linked internally with the planet (through fractal sub-levels), and again linked with the solar system (and more sub-levels) to the galaxy and the universe oscillation.

Dr Noel Huntley

If you enter peace through a fractal wave-knot, then an infinite quantity of charge/energy/spirit that can breath through you, will cancel the loss due to inertia. This is a secret of life. That distribution perfected, without accumulation, not only is the base of abundance in economy, but also an electrical (fractal) symmetry of LIFE.

Daniel Winter

So now I call you to come Home, back into your true relationship with Me, as the entry point in My heart through which My Love moves forth into manifestation. 'Turn back to Love', I say to you, in all of your waking moments and in your dreams. As you recognize My call, you ask Me how to deal with the darkness you see around you. You must withdraw your energy from it. You must recognize your responsibility; you must turn back to Me. From absolutely every perspective on every level of life, dear ones, do not engage it. Do not fight it, seek to destroy it or overcome it. For if you do, the moment you put your attention on it, you are feeding it and giving it life. As you place your attention on darkness you are not seeing yourself. You can only remember who you are by looking at Me, for you are made in My image. You are cells in My heart and the closer we become, the closer you draw to Me, the easier and easier it is to remember who you are.

The Messages from God (through Yael and Doug Powell)

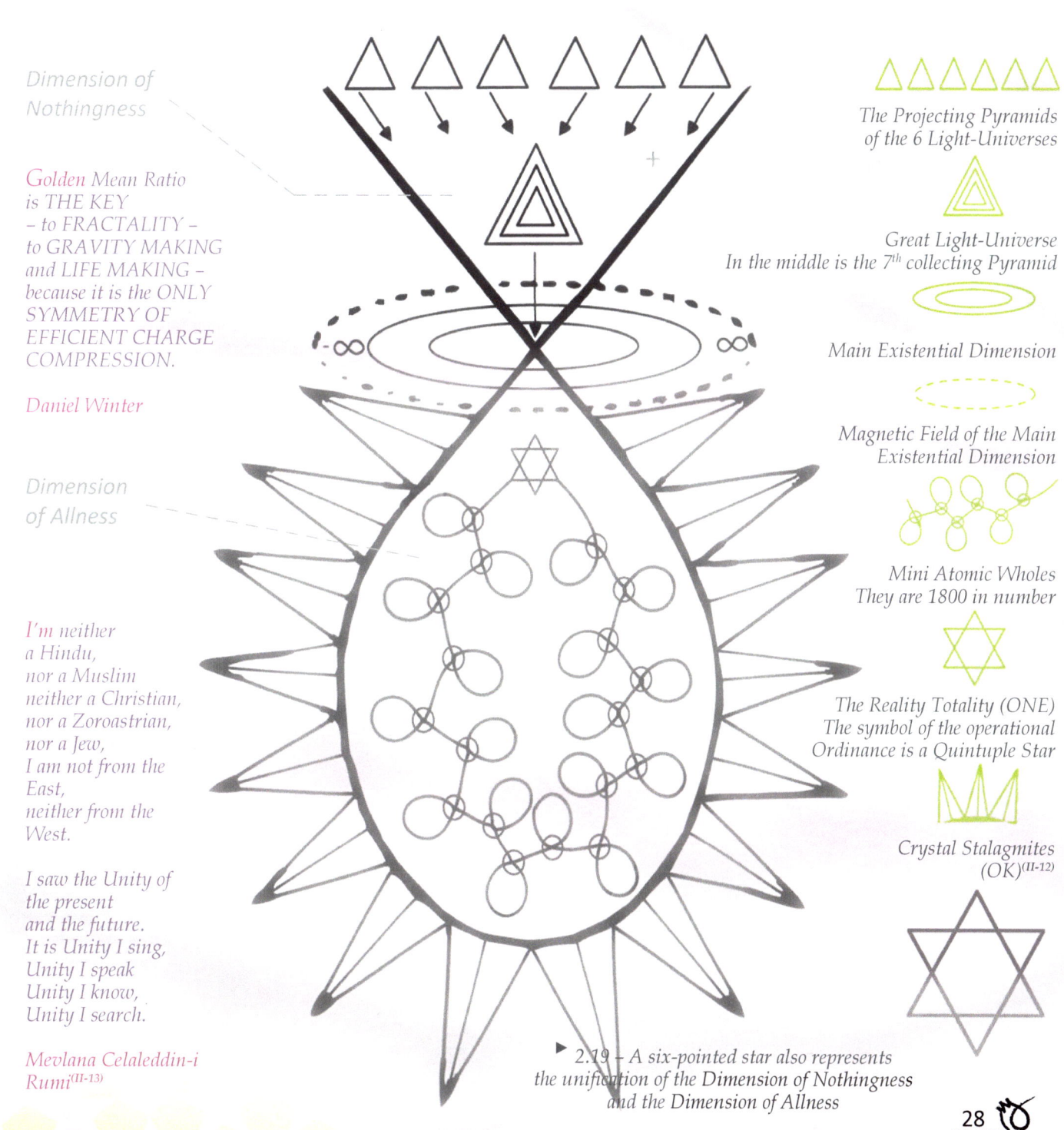

▼ 2.18 – Crystal Gürz(II-11)

Dimension of Nothingness

Golden Mean Ratio is THE KEY – to FRACTALITY – to GRAVITY MAKING and LIFE MAKING – because it is the ONLY SYMMETRY OF EFFICIENT CHARGE COMPRESSION.

Daniel Winter

Dimension of Allness

I'm neither a Hindu, nor a Muslim neither a Christian, nor a Zoroastrian, nor a Jew, I am not from the East, neither from the West.

I saw the Unity of the present and the future. It is Unity I sing, Unity I speak Unity I know, Unity I search.

Mevlana Celaleddin-i Rumi(II-13)

The Projecting Pyramids of the 6 Light-Universes

Great Light-Universe
In the middle is the 7th collecting Pyramid

Main Existential Dimension

Magnetic Field of the Main Existential Dimension

Mini Atomic Wholes
They are 1800 in number

The Reality Totality (ONE)
The symbol of the operational Ordinance is a Quintuple Star

Crystal Stalagmites (OK)(II-12)

▶ 2.19 – A six-pointed star also represents the unification of the Dimension of Nothingness and the Dimension of Allness

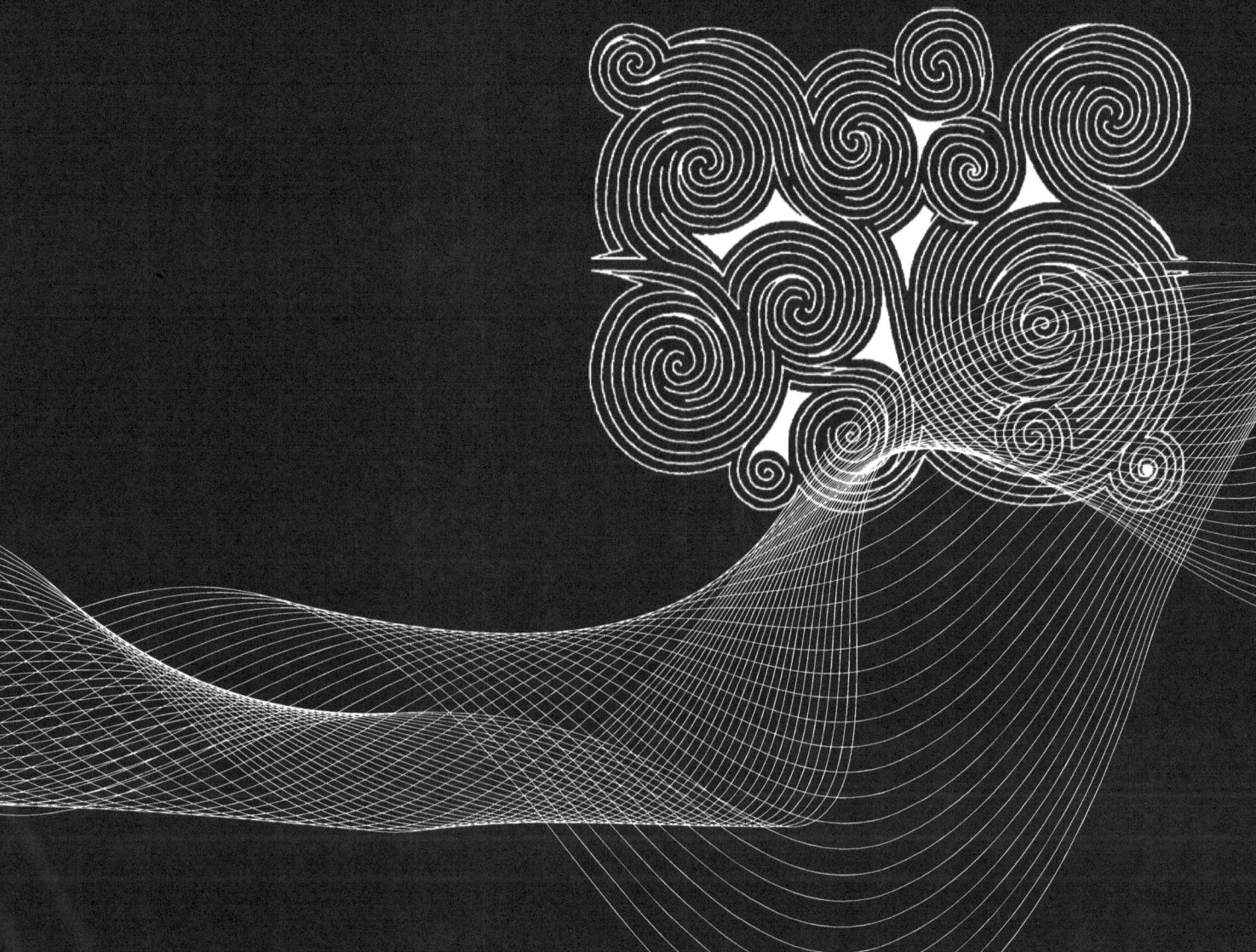

LABYRINTHS

TOWARDS THE FUSION OF THE SELF WITH THE DIVINE 31
PHYSICS OF ASCENSION 32
WALKING TO A HIGHER STATE OF CONSCIOUSNESS 33
HARMONISING THE BRAIN HEMISPHERES 33
INNER JOURNEY 34
VERY OLD AND VERY PRESENT 35
FACING THE UNKNOWN 35

TOWARDS THE FUSION OF THE SELF WITH THE DIVINE

Human experience on this planet is a process of returning to a balanced state of being through transmuting the lower aspects of a fragmented awareness. It is a journey from our inner separation to our inner wholeness inspired by the call of our godly self.

Linearly perceived, there is a separation of our lower self from our higher self expressed as a separation of the self from the not-self, the ego from its environment. If the consciousness does not focus on wholeness, it is then focused on parts, on quantity rather than on unity and quality, and therefore functions in a dualistic manner.

In the *unity consciousness* our mundane self and our divine self are happily married, and all polarities are reconciled.

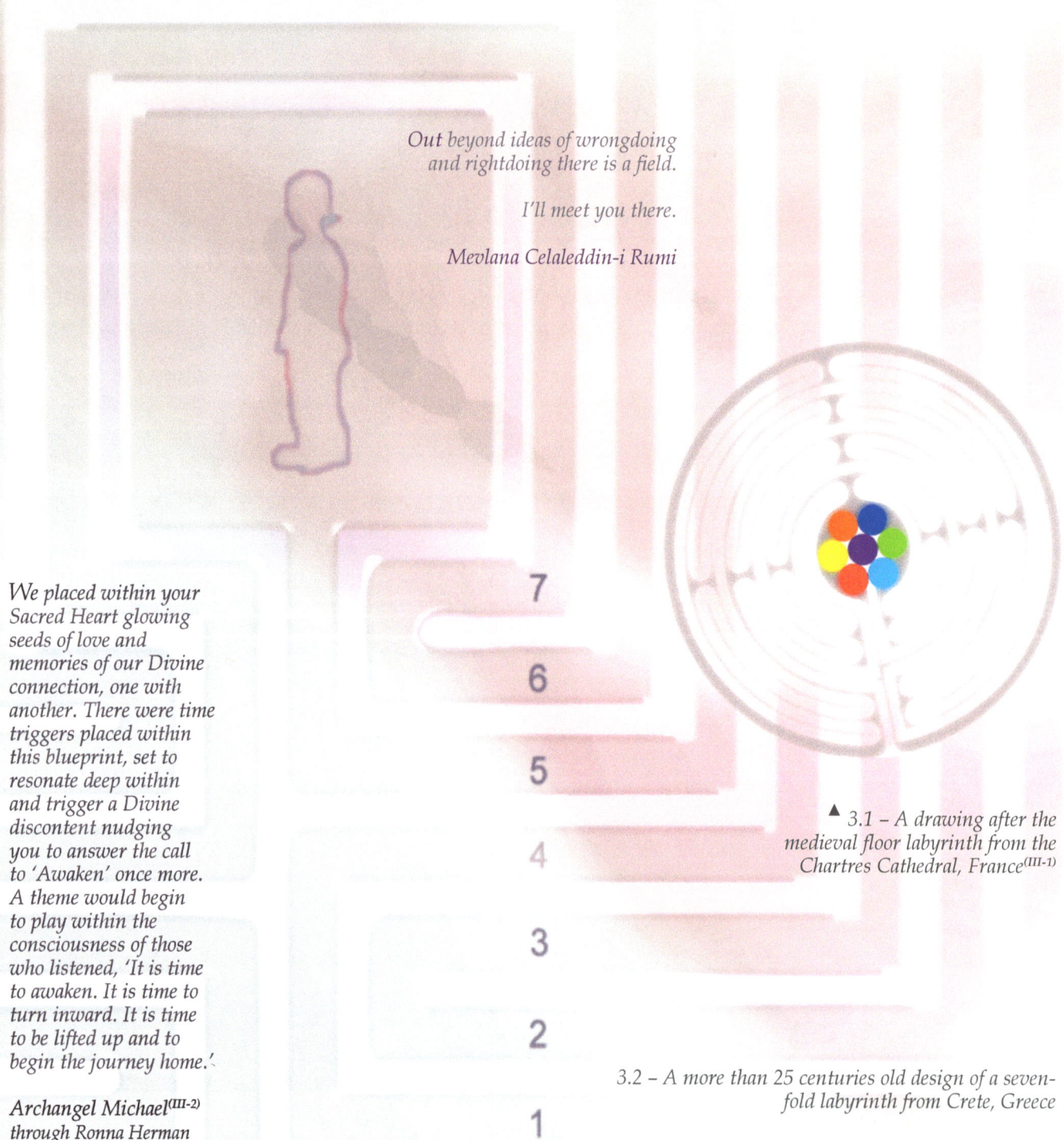

Out beyond ideas of wrongdoing and rightdoing there is a field.

I'll meet you there.

Mevlana Celaleddin-i Rumi

We placed within your Sacred Heart glowing seeds of love and memories of our Divine connection, one with another. There were time triggers placed within this blueprint, set to resonate deep within and trigger a Divine discontent nudging you to answer the call to 'Awaken' once more. A theme would begin to play within the consciousness of those who listened, 'It is time to awaken. It is time to turn inward. It is time to be lifted up and to begin the journey home.'

Archangel Michael[III-2]
through Ronna Herman

▲ 3.1 – A drawing after the medieval floor labyrinth from the Chartres Cathedral, France[III-1]

3.2 – A more than 25 centuries old design of a seven-fold labyrinth from Crete, Greece

PHYSICS OF ASCENSION

One day, You will understand where I am. Who knows, maybe in a point of Time, I and You will meet and will unite with each other. The meaning of this is that I Search for You and You Search for Me.

Great Power, The Knowledge Book
(F47, p 807, par 5)

Intuition is a means of knowing not based on logic and existing context in the mind – in particular as it manifests in feminine energy.

Dr Noel Huntley

According to relativity, no signals can go faster than the speed of light. This is violated by quantum physics which shows that, say, if the frequency of a particle in one location of the universe correlates (resonates) with the frequencies of another particle at a different location, no matter what the distance, both particles are instantly part of a single wave function, meaning that there is an instantaneous connection between them.

Dr Noel Huntley

When an Einstein makes a discovery the inspiration comes from the right-brain intuition and feminine energy. The left-brain logical mind puts it into practice.

Dr Noel Huntley

▼ 3.3 – One of the ideas that led to labyrinth design

Unity consciousness is the evolutionary level acquired after the transcendence of the *duality consciousness*. On that path, understanding how the two brain hemispheres function is a valuable asset.

The left side of the brain is associated with logic, analysis, the use of words and numbers, objectivity, and linear thinking. The right side of the brain characterises a holistic approach, creativity, the use of mental pictures rather than words or numbers, depiction of aesthetic information, spatial perception and visionary thinking.

Consciousness formed through the faculties of the left side of the brain exhibits primal perception as a separation, for it is not able to grasp the wholeness of the phenomena. It takes apart, measures, analyses, and then tries to create a picture by gluing the separate elements into a meaningful whole. Once this happens, the constituents are only associated, but not united into a total which is greater than their sum. Being predominantly rational, we miss the chance to enrich our life in a creative way.

Behind the intuition that operates through the right side of the brain, and the heart centre, there is the physics of resonance. Resonance creates a medium which, through frequency compatibility of the parts involved, enables an effortless transfer of information between them. Hence, Newton's laws of motion lose their value since external forces are not required to achieve movement.

Balancing the functions of both brain hemispheres means moving towards a state of being where we consciously experience the wholeness and interconnections of *All That Is*. The higher frequencies operating through the *unity consciousness* naturally influence the lower frequencies, used by the *duality consciousness*, thus helping them to change.

To speed up that process it is necessary for the *fragmented self*, of the left side of the brain consciousness, to truly recognise itself for what it is. That will consequently heal it and fully harmonise it with the aspect of consciousness which functions through the right brain side. This means that through time, the lower frequencies will transmute under the strength of the higher frequencies, as they are always the context dependent on them. According to the scientist **Dr Noel Huntley**, the result of such a frequency shift in our consciousness is the physics behind what, in a spiritual context, is called ascension.

What do labyrinths have to do with all of this?

▼ *3.4 – Meander patterns more than 10000 years old*

▼ *3.5 – The way to construct a seven–fold labyrinth*

I never came upon any of my discoveries through the process of rational thinking.

Albert Einstein

WALKING TO A HIGHER STATE OF CONSCIOUSNESS

A labyrinth is a geometrical pathway designed either on a two-dimensional or three-dimensional plane. If it is two-dimensional, experience of the labyrinth is achieved by tracing it with a finger. If the labyrinth is part of a garden, church or any other space, then it can be walked through.

The walk is a symbol of a life's journey. Those spiritually awakened, and committed to acquiring higher states of consciousness, are ready to walk through a labyrinth. As involution is compulsory to spiritual self-realisation, an inward spiralling labyrinth's path is a particularly appropriate metaphor for it.

HARMONISING THE BRAIN HEMISPHERES

While meandering through a labyrinth, we constantly make 90° and 180° turns as we are led by its geometry. Changes of direction cause a continuous shifting in activity between the sides of the brain and, being an exercise, help harmonise the work of the brain's hemispheres.

When we arrive at the centre of a labyrinth, and symbolically connect with our divine self, the illusion of separateness dissolves through the realisation of inner wholeness. One is then transformed into the truth that one seeks. This experience refreshes our self-awareness and strengthens our inner light. That personal achievement is our precious gift to our own self and to society.

...To change this reality into a far better one the absolute key to this is full consciousness. In this mode, the present world of duality is transcended and then swiftly replaced by a world of endless possibilities. This all-encompassing realm is connected to the divine parts of you that you currently barely communicate with. Your destiny is to become integrated with all the aspects that are you. Your vastness is to know no bounds!

Galactic Federation of Light[III-3]
through Sheldan Nidle

How many strings tie you to what was? Are you energetically sitting within the matrix of all past thoughts? Is there room for the future in this crowded place?

Gillian MacBeth-Louthan[III-4]
(Quantum Newsletter)

INNER JOURNEY

The essential point for teachers of the ultimate map to successful turning inside-out (labyrinth), is to translate the topological skill learned kinaesthetically from the labyrinth – into what you do INSIDE your heart when you CHOOSE to feel someone outside AS IF they were inside. This is the 'New Sacred Geometry of Compassion'.

Daniel Winter

Daring walk through a labyrinth is cathartic and enlightening. It transmutes our mundane experience into a profound, psychic one where opposing forces, brought about by constant turnings, are recognised and reconciled during the same process. The impurities of the ego-mind are removed, and other inner conflicts are challenged and dissolved, upon reaching the inner nucleus which is symbolised by the centre of the labyrinth. One therefore returns changed forever, after a profound self-encounter. This walk in two directions can be used as a metaphor for entering an incarnation and exiting it, after sufficient enlightenment has been achieved.

All labyrinths, regardless of their geometrical form, serve the same purpose: they take us within ourselves where we can discover the beauty of wholeness, and ourselves as a reflection of it. However, experiences of a labyrinth can vary and depend on the motives and intentions of the searcher. Whatever these intentions may be, walking a labyrinth is a valuable experience in the process of our self-integration.

▼ 3.6 – *A symbol of life's journey among Papago Indians*

> *You get knowledge of roads by getting lost and wandering along roads you never used before.*
>
> Odu Ifa
> (Odu 191)

> *It is only when the lower self is strong and empowered and balanced, that the higher self can unite and become one with the lower self. It is, in many ways, the model of the Twin Flame relationship. And, in fact, we can say that until you have achieved the ability to be 'one' with yourself, you will never be able to be 'one' with another in a Twin Flame relationship.*
>
> Archangel Michael
> through Celia Fenn

VERY OLD AND VERY PRESENT

Labyrinths are scattered around the planet and the earliest are over 3000 years old. It is speculated that they evolved from the meandering shapes prehistoric people carved onto rock walls (Fig. 3.4). The most famous is the Cretan Labyrinth in Knossos, associated with the myth of *Theseus* and the *Minotaur* according to which a *Minotaur* was imprisoned within the labyrinth. Cretan coins, featuring 7-ring labyrinths in both circular and square forms, contributed to its popularity and were, perhaps, the means of spreading the labyrinth to other parts of the world.

Medieval labyrinths served as a substitute for pilgrimages to the Holy Land, because long journeys to the holy city had become too dangerous. Walking a church labyrinth was an act of transformation performed individually, yet within the spirit of a group pilgrimage. The element of belonging to a group served as a reminder that we are on this life journey together.

▶ 3.7 – *A thirteen-spiral maze – illustration by Walter D. Pullen*[III-5]

FACING THE UNKNOWN

A *labyrinth* and a *maze* are not the same. The geometry of a maze is multicursal. A maze presents the seeker with puzzles as to where to go at certain points. It has dead ends, parallel misleading paths and therefore depends on the activities of the left side of the brain in analysing, logical thinking and making conclusions and decisions. Contrary to this, labyrinths take a seeker to the centre without any obstacle except for those in the mind of the seeker. The path is clear, yet not easy.

To walk a labyrinth, one needs a strong spiritual commitment and eagerness to surrender to the unexpected that can emerge from within. Returning to our own centre is a process of merging with the energy of our timeless being. Labyrinths help us to cure and animate suppressed aspects of ourselves, and integrate them in the manner of *unity consciousness*.

Now, at this juncture in the Tree, we see two types of human beings. We see those which are called Holy People: true human beings. And, (secondly) we see those which are physically minded. (Those which still are part of group mind, whose concerns are within the three lowest natures within the human ability: physical survival, basic sexuality and struggling to overcome self. These are the first three spheres of human being and are the spheres of those that we term as 'unaware people.) They have not yet discovered the power of heart, or the Truth of the Sacred Word which is invested in them, or the Great Vision of Spirit which gave them birth, or their very Connection to All.

Human beings that have learned the Seven Facets of Self are conscious. Once human beings have risen unto giving their life in service to all Relations, they are Holy People.

CANUPA
(Empowers Respect for Mitakuye Oyasin)

You are not going to move completely into the right brain and exist over there. You are going to be blending the two together where you can quantify god. Imagine it this way: god is the infinite and exists in the right part of your brain, for you are god, and the left part of the brain is the part that pretends to be a human, the part that quantifies everything and figures everything out by putting it in neat little boxes to give to your children so they can give it to their children, and so forth. You have done such a good job that you actually believe you are human. That is so funny on our side of the veil. You teach everyone that you are human, when in fact you are spirits playing a game. You have forgotten the veil. That is a testament of your own creative abilities.

The Group[III-6]
through Steve Rother

Do you know who you are? We do. You are the greatest angels that have ever lived. It is our honour to offer you only three reminders:

1. Treat each other with respect of the highest degree, for you are looking in the eyes of God.

2. Nurture one another at every opportunity, for you are nurturing yourselves.

3. Re-member that it is a wonderful Game and play well together.

The Group
through Steve Rother

Trying creates impossibilities. *Letting go* creates what is desired.

Stalking Wolf
(Apache Elder)

COSMIC DIAGRAMS

MANDALAS 39
JANTRAS 40
SURRENDERING TO THE GEOMETRY OF SILENCE 41
ISLAMIC PATTERNS 42
LINES ARE GUIDED BY NUMBERS 42
PARTICLE AND WHOLE BELONG
TO THE SAME REALITY 43
ENERGETIC SIGNATURE OF CREATION

MANDALAS

Mandalas are abstract circular patterns which have been used in spiritual practices of many cultures, since the beginning of time, as an indispensable aid in meditation and a promoter of healing. It is believed that they facilitate purification of the soul and elevate it to a state of unity with its divine source.

Mandala is a Sanskrit word, meaning *circle* or *community*. For Buddhists it is an archetypal template, and a graphic cosmic symbol comprising manifold meanings. Typically, it is in the form of a circle enclosed by a squared palace with four gates where every detail is of profound significance. It may also have either a geometric or figurative indication of deities. Generally, all *mandalas* convey the same message and that is to return to the centre, to the essence of the self.

The tapestry of pictorial stories, brought about by the symbolic use of geometry, figurative motifs, and colours, takes an aspirant on the archetypal journey. The aim of such a journey is to rediscover the inner spot of stillness which is our inherent link with the One, with the Source. Thus, the *mandala* is a sacred meditational guidance on how to attain peace, purity and wisdom. It inspires us during the process of our spiritual realisation and stimulates our connection with the Divine.

In everything there is an expansion from the Centre outwards. It is the same with the Universe, too. The closer you are to the Center, the more You benefit from the influence of that Center.

You see the rings around a stone thrown into the water, but You can not see the rings reaching the shore. But those rings are not lost, they are there. You can not see them due to the insufficiency of the Bodily capacity in the Real Realm.

In fact, You cannot deny the things You do not see, the things You do not know. If You keep a cup of water for a long time, some sediment forms at the final ring of the water zone as a result of evaporation. This, too is an example of expanding from the Center outwards.

The Knowledge Book
(F16, p 240, par 1-3)

Mandalas are similar to telephone numbers in that you can connect yourself with the actual divine qualities that they represent by attuning to their energy. Even if you do not know the meanings of the numbers and the colors, the divine qualities that are represented by symbols affect changes in the glands through the activity of the optic nerve and attunement occurs in intuition and psychic sensitivity.

Angels of Visual Art
(Tapum[IV-1])

Stop talking and thinking, and there is nothing you will not be able to know.

Seng Ts'an[IV-2]

▼ 4.1 – Every mandala is an invitation for interdimensional travel

JANTRAS

> *I had to abandon the idea of the superordinate position of the ego. ... I saw that everything, all paths I had been following, all steps I had taken, were leading back to a single point – namely, to the mid-point. It became increasingly plain to me that the mandala is the centre. It is the exponent of all paths. It is the path to the centre, to individuation.*
>
> Carl Gustav Jung[IV-3]

In Indian *tantric* tradition, an equivalent to the *mandala* is called *yantra*. *Yantra* is also a Sanskrit word meaning *to support, to sustain*. The *tantric yantra* is a geometrical composition of archetypal value used in meditation or the worshipping of a deity. *Yantras* usually have *mantras*[IV-4] inscribed on them. When pronounced correctly, *mantras* act like the soul of the *yantra*. This combination of visual and audio components, as two synergistic dynamics, transforms the geometrical pattern into a unique power diagram.

The *yantra* is a valuable assistant in the quest of experiencing oneness through the process of self-transcendence. Its geometrical vocabulary has rich religious and cosmological connotations. Every *yantra* is a sacred house of a deity. The specific nature of a venerated deity is translated through a particular geometry into energy perceivable on the mundane level – hence the *yantra*'s contribution towards the merging of the sacred and the profane. A *yantra* provides the bridge for Man on his inner journey towards reaching the godly self.

The circular shape of the *yantra* reflects the nature of cosmic structures as perceived by Indians. According to them, the basic cosmic principle is a concentric expansion and contraction of the One, the infinite primordial potential. Therefore, the circle is an ideal form to represent that process.

Other geometrical elements used in a *yantra* composition are dots, triangles and squares. The dot at the centre of a *yantra* symbolises a starting point, the Source. As a focus of meditation, it is also a symbol of our target – the proper centring of ourselves in the process of awakening. The dot, present within cosmic and mental contexts simultaneously, reveals multilevelled symbolism of every *yantra*. By providing the medium for the fusion of these levels, the cosmic diagram becomes a concealed diagram of our psyche and our body. The *yantra* enables us to experience the symmetry of Creation expressed in the saying: *as is within, so is without; as is above, so is below.*

▲ 4.2 – *Sri yantra* celebrates the union of opposing forces shown as an interplay of five downward-pointing triangles – representing the female principle (Shakti) and four upward-pointing triangles – representing the male principle (Shiva). United, as nine triangles, they create a cosmic field represented by 43 smaller triangles, each one of them being associated with one deity.

The sound of Brahman is Om.
At the end of Om there is silence.
It is silence of joy.

Gautama Buddha[IV-5]
(The Dhammapada)

▲ 4.3 – The geometry of the OM (AUM) sound vibration is a pattern that corresponds to Sri yantra

Spirituality could very well be defined as the multidimensional physics of inner space.

Dr Noel Huntley

40

SURRENDERING TO THE GEOMETRY OF SILENCE

During meditation, the geometrical pattern of either the *mandala* or the *yantra* is brought into a resonance with the geometry of our subtle bodies. That rapport aligns our energy with the higher vibrations of the rhythmic unity encoded into the symbolism of the *mandala*'s or *yantra*'s design. Since thoughts are words, and words are aspects of sounds, real silence of mind is achieved only if the mind is void of words. Such a meditative state, wherein we quieten our mind and our thinking process, opens to us a whole new potential for existence by activating the power of silence.

It is a great task to control our thoughts and emotions, and a great evolutionary challenge to conquer our own minds. The reward is divine, for a silent mind provides a mirror for eternity. It is a fountain of endless joy and love.

By learning to voluntarily stop our thinking and just BE, we gradually discover how to awaken our deep inner knowing, trusting it fully. When that trust is complete, there is nothing which we will not be able to understand and manifest through our blissful heart.

From the analysis of the Energies carried by each particle of Light, We have reached such unknown and Unthought of results that in accordance with this View, it is presumed that only Our Thoughts bring Us to Existence.

The Knowledge Book
(F16, p 245, par 1)

Focus, and attention, is the power to hold a wave node (seed) fixed within the flux, like choosing the note (node) by putting a finger on the fret of the guitar string – the shape of the wave, which is given the chance to stand, is chosen by the places of STILLNESS.

Daniel Winter

You cannot know or feel our Father/Mother God or the Creator through an idea or a nebulous thought or theory. It isn't enough to just know or think about God, you must feel the Essence, the overwhelming love of the Creator within your Sacred Heart Center. Then there is no doubt within your mind that you have reconnected with your God-Self and the Oneness of all Creation. The mind can be a competent servant, but without its connection to the Sacred Heart, it can be a controlling and destructive master. That is why it is imperative that you activate and empower both the Sacred Heart and the Sacred Mind.

Archangel Michael
through Ronna Herman

Just remain in the centre, watching. And then forget that you are there.

Lao Tzu

▲ 4.4 – Kali yantra – *a yantra of primordial energy*

▶ 4.5 – Rhythm with no end

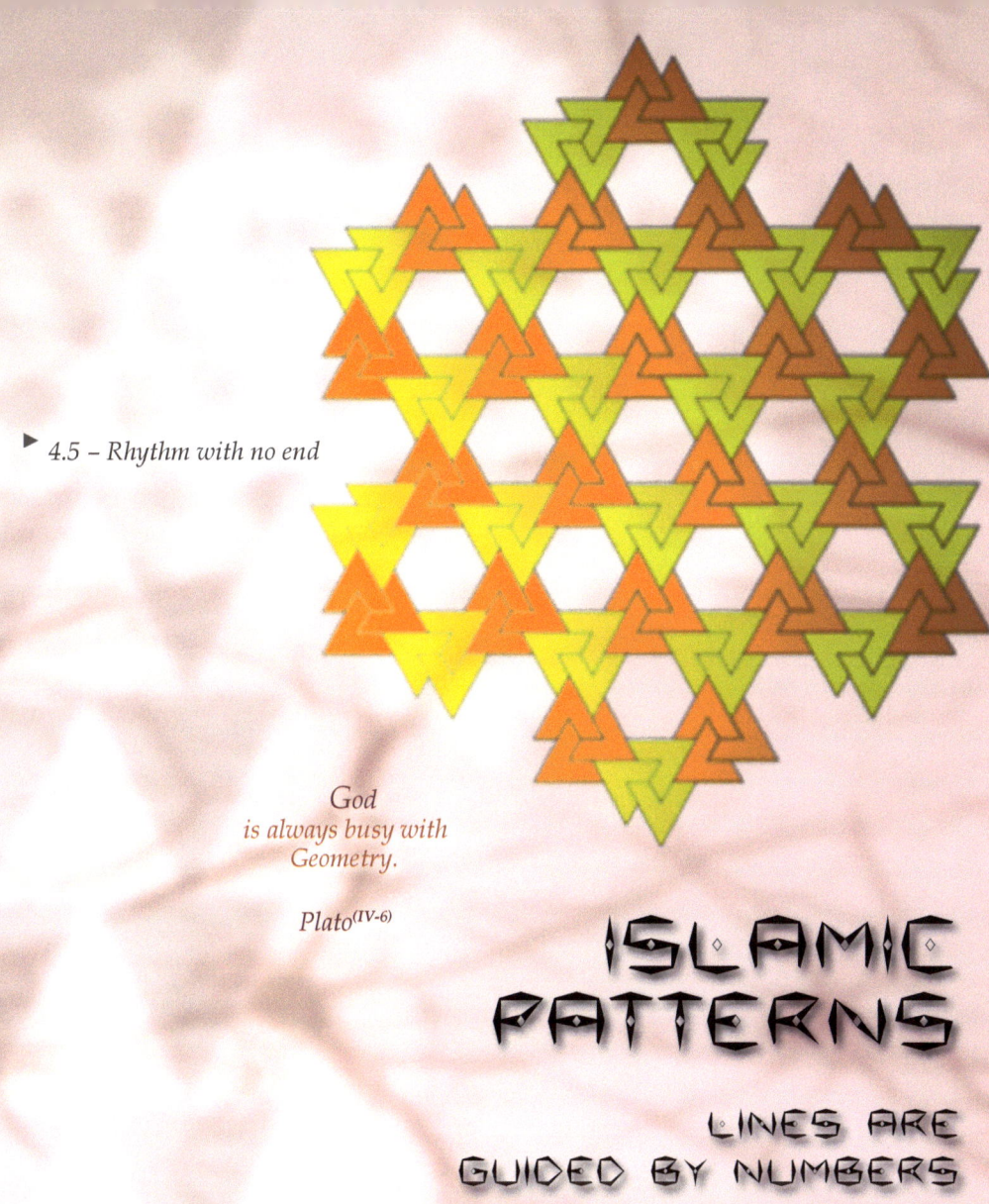

*God
is always busy with
Geometry.*

Plato[(IV-6)]

ISLAMIC PATTERNS

LINES ARE GUIDED BY NUMBERS

Following the wisdom and teachings of their sacred book, *The Quran,* Islamic cultures avoided figurative motifs in their decorative arts for a long time. In the search for the meaning of the Supreme One and in the yearning to suggest its endlessness to this world of the finite and ephemeral, Islamic craftsmen pondered over the realm of lines and mastered their expressive potential. Lines are guided by numbers and numbers have divine origin according to Islamic belief.

The anthropomorphic appearance of *Allah* is not indicated in *the Quran.* Thus the word *Allah,* unlike the word *God,* does not have a plural or gender. Subsequently, every effort to grasp and visually present that Supreme Power inevitably leads to the abstract. Behind human, animal and plant bodies, Islamic artists discerned geometry as the skeleton of these forms. Thus geometry, which works like a matrix, gives birth to all and connects all. Islamic patterns represent an immense beauty of life and form understood at their metaphysical level. Since these patterns spread without limits, they actually talk about One illustrating One's infinite harmony, rhythm and omnipresence.

▲ 4.6 – *The yantra denoting the knowledge aspect of the supreme goddess* Shakti, *is celebrated as a cluster of her emanations*

One can see the forest or the trees, but never both at the same time. Therefore, perception is always singular, but in a sequential context it creates an illusion of diversity. This is the (in)famous 'maya' of the eastern traditions, turning waves into particles. The day we stop giving names to things (knowledge of 'good and bad'), we may return to pure Spirit as the cause of everything.

Frank van den Bovenkamp
(Heart Coherence team)

PARTICLE AND WHOLE BELONG TO THE SAME REALITY

Primordial Power, the One and Only, the Eternal, Absolute – *Allah*, in Islamic art is depicted through geometry. In this art tradition, the Creation is seen as a reflection of the Supreme Geometer's Mind. Thus the essence of existence and higher everlasting meanings are sought through numbers and geometry. In an ultimate picture of life, according to an Islamic artist, the symmetry of abstract geometric forms and a rhythm of engaged and non-engaged space connect the variety of the many into an orderly whole of One.

Parts are meaningful only if the whole that encompasses them exists. A particle and the whole belong to the same reality. Islamic artists understand the timeless principles of the Creation and speak about them in mathematical terms in their works. They reduce the visible form to its geometrical core and, through the seductive interweaving of lines, slide into the world of the inner and beyond time.

So, the pictures that Islamic artists are busy with are the pictures of their own divine essence, the pictures of their soul. That is exactly what *Allah* taught them and led them to discover – the ability of geometry to guide us Home. Our soul recognises messages of geometrical patterns. In resonance with their archetypal values, on the waves of primordial longing, the soul rides back to its source.

Listen, open a window to God and begin to delight yourself by gazing upon Him through the opening.

The business of love is to make that window in the heart…

Mevlana Celaleddin-i Rumi

By the entering into Effect of the entire functions of the 7 Layers of a Brain, The Brain goes out of the Effect of the mechanism of Influences. And afterwords, Mental Functions enter into Effect in Brain activities. The Mind is the Unification of the Essence Consciousness and the Brain Power.

The Mind is a Power potential opening to each other the Sacred Partitions present within the Brain. This connects the Consciousness and Realisation layers to each other. And Thought provides becoming Aware and becoming Conscious. And in this way, Creative Intelligence enters into Effect.

Vedia Bülent (Önsü) Çorak
(Light)

ENERGETIC SIGNATURE OF CREATION

4.7 – *The geometrical integrity of the endlessness, described by Islamic artists*

Islamic artists are scientists at the same time. In their work they externalise the logic and order of the inner realm. The inner realm is only an expression of cosmological orderliness and hence Islamic artists expose to the world the geometry of the Spirit. However strong their passion to beautify the living environment is, they do not try to copy nature by employing the so-called realistic style. They are not after imitating it but after understanding the energetic signatures of Creation. These signatures are many-layered, having as much depth as one is ready to search for and discover. The potential is endless.
Plurality is organised through the numerical laws of One.

Throughout the centuries, Islamic art has been passing the message that multiplicity is just an expression of unity, of God, of the magnificent beauty of One.

The world is made up of waves and sacred proportions…

Waves are drawn to FOCUS and automatically sort themselves and agree to sustain via Sacred Geometry. They align to still points, creating 'CHARGE', 'stasis', 'ecstasy', 'tingle', 'pure intention' and LIFE-FORCE.

Daniel Winter

Peace is a name for the energy centering force which fractality produces!

Daniel Winter

Beloveds, let go of the energies of judgment and scarcity. Let go of old self-limiting beliefs that no longer serve your greatest good. Keep an open mind and stretch your beliefs to allow your consciousness to expand as you tap into the cosmic libraries of Divine wisdom. Attune to your God Self when you strive to discern what is your highest truth. Listen to the wisdom of your soul/heart centre, and allow your mind to tap into the Essence of higher truth which is stored within your brain structure. You came forth with all the wisdom, information, talents and abilities you would ever need to create a paradise on Earth. It is time to reclaim your Divine Heritage as a powerful Co-creator of beauty, joy, abundance and peaceful co-existence with all the diverse facets of Creation.

Archangel Michael
through Ronna Herman

4.8 – *Gazing into infinity – a hexagonal decorative motif used in Islamic art and craft*

SPIRALS

I-1   Sándor Kabai is a mechanical engineer specialising in aviation and manufacturing technology. He is a member of the Geometry and Space Research Team – an inter-disciplinary group hosted by the Academy of Sciences and various universities in Hungary. On his website complex mathematical graphics can be found; www.kabai.hu

I-2   Reproduced from the book Hidden Nature by Alick Bartholomew, by kind permission from the author

I-3   Illustrations: a – Daniel Erdely, b – Daniel Erdely and Rinus Roelofs. Find more about the *Spidron system* at: www.szinhaz.hu/edan/spidronatlanta and www.spidron.hu

I-4   Democritus (Δημόκριτος, 450BC-370BC), an ancient Greek philosopher, believed that all matter consisted of imperishable and indivisible elements which he called *atoma*. He laughed easily and a lot, and became known as the *laughing philosopher*.

I-5   Daniel Winter, a writer and lecturer in the areas of electrical engineering, psychophysiology (the origin of languages), computer animation in multimedia and non-linear energy source technologies. Winter developed superior technology for measuring coherent emotions in the heart *(HeartTuner*, also called *BlissTuner)*. In his research and practical work he bridges the physical with the metaphysical; www.fractalfield.com

I-6   Albrecht Dürer (1471-1528), was a German painter, engraver, wood carver and mathematician of Hungarian ancestry. His work *Melancholia I* features a 4th order *magic square* believed to be seen in European art for the first time. During his lifetime Dürer produced one book on fortification (1527), and one on geometry and perspective *(The Painter's Manual,* 1525), while his studies of human proportion appeared after 1528. His famous woodcuts and numerous self-portraits reveal his exquisite sense of detail and realism.

I-7   *Ammonites* appeared during the Devonian Era. The origin of their name is related to the word *Ammon* (also spelled *Amun,* an ancient Egyptian God), who is pictured as having a ram's horn (which look like *ammonites*) behind each ear.

I-8   Frank van den Bovenkamp, *Heart Coherence team*; www.heartcoherence.com

I-9   *The Knowledge Book,* given through Vedia Bülent (Önsü) Çorak, contains the frequencies of all sacred books, revealed to our planet so far, together with the frequency of the *Mighty Energy Focal Point*. It is a *Universal Constitution* of the *Lordly order* also called the *Golden Book of the Golden Age* or the *Book of Truth*. All references relate to hardcover book (Second Edition, January 1998) www.dkb-mevlana.org.tr

I-10 Lao Tzu (老子, 570BC-490BC – though many believe he never existed), was born in Ch'u (the present-day Henan Province in China). Lao Tzu literally means *Old Master*. He was a contemporary of Confucius in China as well as of Plato and Socrates in Greece, and Buddha in India. Lao Tzu is the founder of *Taoism*.

I-11 Illustration based on the work from Michael S. Schneider's book *A Beginner's Guide to Constructing the Universe – the Mathematical Archetypes of Nature, Art, and Science*; www.constructingtheuniverse.com

FRACTALS

II-1 Ibrahim F. Karim, PhD, Egyptian architect, the father of the new science of BioGeometry™. With Rawya Karim, MA, he founded the *BioGeometrical Systems Institute Company* in 1993 as a design centre for research and implementation of BioGeometry™. More information about their work in the book *Messages behind Shapes*; www.biogeometry.com

II-2 Jain, born in Australia to Lebanese parents, is the author of 12 books and 6 DVDs on ancient knowledge in the areas of *Vedic mathematics*, *magic squares*, *sacred geometry*, *divine proportion* and the *Platonic solids*. As a theatrical director he developed a maths enrichment programme for schools called *MatheMagics*. Through a performance called *The Theatre of the Holy Numbers*, mathematics is taught through a play in which actors wear elaborate costumes. Jain has been lecturing in schools and universities around Australia for more than 15 years. He authored many exhibitions on mathematical art, and is also a healer/herbalist and muralist; www.jainmathemagics.com

II-3 Illustration by Daniel Winter (www.fractalfield.com; www.goldenmean.info) and Frank Van Den Bovenkamp from *Heart Coherence team* (www.heartcoherence.com)

II-4 *The chaos game* can be performed on any polygon. The Method shown has been described by Michael F. Barnsley

II-5 Yael and Doug Powell, *Messages from God;* www.circleoflight.net

II-6 For information on *phyllotaxis,* see chapter *SPIRALS,* page 10

II-7 Noel Huntley, PhD, English scientist with a background in physics and doctorates in psychology and parapsychology, also a talented painter and musician, with a keen interest in computers. He has developed the foundation for a spiritual science as well as for the physics of a higher dimensional consciousness. Some of his books are: *ET and ALIENS: Who Are They? And Why Are They Here?; The Scientific Principles of Spiritual Enslavement* and *Attainment of Superior Physical Abilities and the New Science of Body Motion.* His website *Beyond Duality* is a collection of articles on variety of topics, like evolution, the nature of time, ascension, consciousness, holographic civilisation, fractals, types of physics and the theory of one; www.users.globalnet.co.uk/~noelh

II-8 Celia Fenn, holds an MA and a PhD in English Literature and also studied music and art. She is a medium, photographer, writer, and the author of *A Guide to Complementary Therapies in South*

Africa. Fenn works with Indigo adults, teenagers and children, and has developed a programme to assist them in their transition from Indigo to Crystal consciousness. Her articles appear in magazines in the USA, UK, Germany and New Zealand; www.starchildglobal.com

II-9 Vedia Bülent (Önsü) Çorak, *The Knowledge Book,* Fascicule 23, pages 347, 353.

II-10 Vedia Bülent (Önsü) Çorak, *The Knowledge Book,* Fascicule 10, pages 143-147

II-11 Vedia Bülent (Önsü) Çorak, *The Knowledge Book,* Fascicule 35, pages 568-574

II-12 OK is a measuring unit for distance. 1OK=1.5 billion kilometres. Each stalagmite of the *crystal Gürz* is 133,000OK long (Vedia Bülent (Önsü) Çorak, *The Knowledge Book,* Fascicule 53, page 932).

II-13 Mevlana Celaleddin-i Rumi (1207-1273) worldwide celebrated poet and Sufi mystic. Just like Zoroaster, he was born in the Persian city of Balkh (present-day North Afghanistan). A 3000-year-history makes Balkh one of the oldest cities in the world. Many cultures left their mark on it: Buddhists, Greeks with Alexander the Great, Arabs, and Mongols with Genghis Khan. Escaping from the Mongols in 1225, Rumi's father settled with his family in the city of Konya in Anatolia (Turkey), then part of the Turkish Seljuk Empire. Rumi was the founder of the Mevlevi Sufi order, a mystical brotherhood of Islam. His most famous work is a poetical interpretation of themes from *The Quran*, in the Pahlavi language, known as the *Mesnevi*.

LABYRINTHS

III-1 All attempts by the author to reveal the originator, and to contact the originator/guardian of this figure, have been to no avail. The same applies to the illustrations featured in the figures 3.3, 34, 3.5 and 3.6. If you have information about them, please contact the author via the publishers in order to give proper acknowledgement.

III-2 Ronna Herman is an internationally known lecturer and author of eight books. The books and messages transmitted to her from Archangel Michael have been translated into most major languages and read around the world. You may contact her at: RonnaStar@earthlink.net, www.ronnastar.com

III-3 Sheldan Nidle is a representative and lecturer for the *Galactic Federation of Light*. He founded the *Planetary Activation Organization (PAO)* in November 1997; www.paoweb.com

III-4 Gillian MacBeth-Louthan is a clairvoyant psychic, a metaphysical teacher, messenger and internationally known medium. For over 35 years she has been working with the *Councils of Light, Mary Magdalene, Merlin, White Buffalo Calf Woman, Mother Mary, Pleiadians* and many other energies of the Christ Light; www.thequantumawakening.com

III-5 Walter D. Pullen graduated in computer science from *The University of Washington,* USA, in 1992. His interests are vast and range from astrology, spirituality, labyrinths, computer graphics, computer games and music, to mountain climbing. As an astrologer, he created the freeware astrology programme *Astrolog*. He also reads *Tarot cards and Runes;* www.astrolog.org/home.htm

III-6 Messages from The GROUP first came to Steve Rother in 1996. Translated into 11 languages so far, they have filled several books since (see the back cover). The monthly *Beacons of Light – Reminders from Home* have been translated into 21 languages and presented at the United Nations five times; www.lightworker.com

COSMIC DIAGRAMS

IV-1   Messages from Angels; www.star-knowledge.net

IV-2   Seng Ts'an (520-606) was an ancient Chinese sage, the third patriarch of Zen Buddhism in China.

IV-3   Karl Gustav Jung (1875-1961) was the Swiss psychiatrist and founder of analytical psychology who, in his early career, collaborated with Sigmund Freud. His broad interests included philosophy of both the West and the East, sociology, religion, astrology, mythology, art, literature, alchemy and dreams. Jung coined terms, used in analytical psychology, such as: *archetype, synchronicity, collective unconscious, psychological complex,* the *Anima* and the *Animus*.

IV-4   *Mantra* is a Sanskrit word meaning *instrument of thought* (man = to think, tra = tool). It is a syllable or poem, usually in Sanskrit, employed in spiritual practices. Its purpose is believed to be the aligning of the vibrations of the person who uses it, with higher sources that would result in the purification of his/her body and mind. The correct pronunciation of a *mantra* is essential since its power is considered to be in its sound. The process of repeating a *mantra* is called *chanting*.

IV-5   Gautama Buddha was named Siddhārtha Gautama at birth and lived in ancient India between c563BC-c483BC. He was a spiritual teacher and the historical founder of Buddhism. In a general sense, the word *Buddha* can be used for anyone who becomes enlightened by spiritual cultivation – the purification of the body and mind, the discovery of the true nature of reality, the transcendence of suffering, and the practicing of a moral life through the virtues of the *middle path* and the *noble eightfold path*. *The Dhammapada*, the wisdom of Gautama Buddha consisting of 423 verses in Pali, was recorded some four centuries after Buddha lived.

IIV-6   Plato (Πλάτων, 427BC-347BC), is considered one of the most significant ancient Greek philosophers. Plato's Academy was built in 428BC, in Athens, on a site continuously inhabited since prehistoric times. The philosophical school gained fame thanks to the Neoplatonists. It existed for more than seven centuries, before Emperor Justinian closed it in the year 347AD.

Front cover: Detail of the *Dimension of the All-Truthful*
Graphic design of the book: zodrag@gmail.com

BIBLIOGRAPHY

- ANTI-GRAVITY & THE WORLD GRID, edited by David Hatcher Childress; Adventures Unlimited Press
- THE ANCIENT SECRETS OF THE FLOWER OF LIFE, Volume 1 & 2 by Drunvalo Melchizedek; Sedona Color Graphics
- A BEGINNER'S GUIDE TO CONSTRUCTING THE UNIVERSE – The mathematical archetypes of Nature, Art, and Science a voyage from 1 to 10 by Michael S. Schneider; Harper Perennial, a division of Harper Collins Publishers
- CELTIC SPIRALS – handbook by Sheila Sturrock; Guild of Master Craftsman Publication Ltd
- FENG SHUI – The Traditional Oriental Way to Enhance Your Life by Stephen Skinner; Siena book, an imprint of Parragon
- THE FRACTAL GEOMETRY OF NATURE by Benoit B. Mandelbrot; W. H. Freeman and Company, New York
- THE GEOMETRY OF ART AND LIFE by Matila Ghyka; Dover Publications, inc. New York
- HIDDEN NATURE – The Startling Insights of Viktor Schauberger by Alick Bartholomew; Floris Books
- THE IMPLOSIONS' GRAND ATTRACTOR – Sacred Geometry & Coherent Emotion; assembled, Edited & Distributed from Daniel Winter's writing by Implosion Group
- ISLAMIC PATTERNS – An Analytical and Cosmological Approach by Keith Critchlow; Thames and Hudson, London
- JUST SIX NUMBERS – The Deep Forces that Shape the Universe by Martin Rees; Weidenfeld & Nicolson – London
- THE KNOWLEDGE BOOK – Messages received and transformed into writing by Vedia Bülent (Önsü) Çorak; World Brotherhood Union Mevlana Supreme Foundation, Istanbul
- L' ASTROLOGIE SACRE – Miroir de la Grande Tradition, Frederic Lionel; Editions du Rocher, Monaco
- LET THE NUMBERS GUIDE YOU – The Spiritual Science of Numerology by Shiv Charan Singh; O Books, Winchester, UK; New York, USA
- MAGIC SYMBOLS by Frederick Goodman; Brian Trodd Publishing House Limited
- THE MASTER MASONS OF CHARTRES by John James; West Grinstead Publishing
- NATURE'S NUMBERS – Discovering Order And Pattern In The Universe by Ian Stewart; Weidenfeld & Nicolson – London
- NUMEROLOGY with Tantra, Ayurveda, and Astrology – A Key to Human Behaviour by Harish Johari; Destiny Books, Rochester, Vermont
- ORDER IN SPACE – A Design Source Book by Keith Critchlow; Thames and Hudson, London
- PATTERN AND DESIGN WITH DYNAMIC SYMMETRY – How to Create Art Deco Geometrical Design by Edward B. Edwards; Dover Publications, inc, New York
- RANDOMNESS by Deborah J. Bennett; Harvard University Press, Cambridge, Massachusetts, London England
- SACRED GEOMETRY by Miranda Lundy; Wooden Books Ltd
- SACRED GEOMETRY – Philosophy and practice by Robert Lawlor; Thames and Hudson
- SECRETS OF ANCIENT AND SACRED PLACES – The world's Mysterious Heritage by Paul Devereux; Brockhampton Press, London
- SUNLIGHT ON WATER – A Manual for Soul-full Living – The One With No Names through Flo Aeveia Magdalena
- SYMMETRY IN CHAOS – A Search for Pattern in mathematics, Art and Nature by Michael Field and Martin Golubitsky; Oxford University Press
- THE JOY OF PI by David Plather; Bath Press Colourbooks, Glasgow
- THE SECRET SCIENCE OF ECSTASY AND IMMORTALITY – IMPLOSION by Daniel Winter
- THE TRUE POWER OF WATER – Healing And Discovering Ourselves by Masaru Emoto; Beyond Words Publishing, Inc., Hillsboro, Oregon
- YANTRA – The Tantric Symbol of Cosmic Unity by Madhu Khanna; Thames and Hudson

Copyright © Milena 2015
All rights reserved.

No part of this publication may be reproduced, stored in or introduced into a retrieval system, or transmitted, in any form, or by any means (electronic, mechanical, photocopying, recording, or otherwise) without the prior written permission of the copyright owner.

Published by
M PUBLISHING
www.memento13.com

A catalogue record for this book is available from the British Library

ISBN
978-1-909323-12-4

www.ingramcontent.com/pod-product-compliance
Lightning Source LLC
Chambersburg PA
CBHW040057160426
43192CB00002B/101